PILGRIMS

AND

PATRIOTS

****

The Radical Christian Roots of American Democracy and Freedom

****

EDDIE L. HYATT

HYATT PRESS * 2016

Publish, and set up a standard; publish and conceal not (Jeremiah 50:2)

PILGRIMS AND PATRIOTS:
The Radical Christian Roots of American Democracy & Freedom
By Eddie L. Hyatt
© 2016 by Hyatt International Ministries, Incorporated
ALL RIGHTS RESERVED.

Published by Hyatt Press
A Subsidiary of Hyatt Int'l Ministries, Incorporated

Mailing Address (2016)
P.O. Box 3877
Grapevine, TX 76099-3877

Internet Addresses
Email: dreddiehyatt@gmail.com
Web Site: www.eddiehyatt.com
Social Media: Eddie L. Hyatt

Cover and Book Design by Susan C. Hyatt

Cover Images
Top Left: Rev. Robert Hunt gives thanks at Cape Henry, VA in April of 1607. NPS Image.
Top Right: The-Pilgrims-Landing-Nov, by Dr. Mike Haywood
Bottom: Washington Crossing the Delaware, by Emanuel Leutz, in the Metropolitan Museum of Art, NYC.

Unless otherwise indicated, all Scripture quotations
are taken from the New Kings James Version of the Bible. ©
1979, 1980, 1982 by Thomas Nelson, Inc. Publishers.

ISBN: 978-1-888435-55-9

Printed in the United States of America

Endorsements

"I believe you have put together an outstanding book, and I am more than delighted to supply the following endorsement for your use. 'Eddie Hyatt has captured the heart of the Christian faith which animated the founding of this great Nation in which we live. I commend *Pilgrims and Patriots* as a must-read for those who wish to denigrate and downgrade the spiritual roots of our Nation.'"

Pat Robertson, President of CBN, Host of The 700 Club

"I have known Eddie Hyatt and his wife Sue since the early 70s. I am impressed with their diligent research and discipline to write. Their heart's pure motivation is to aid the body of Christ by discovering truth that pulls back the veil of tradition and dogma that prevents the church from moving forward. Their writing is uncompromising, bold and challenging. That takes courage, which they have. They live the righteous life they write about.

Dr. Bill Kaiser, Times of Refreshing, Fort Worth, TX

"In his latest book, Dr. Eddie Hyatt takes us back to our roots. He expertly documents how the vision for a new nation 'under God' waned before God breathed on the nation in what we know as the First Great Awakening in the 1700s, which ultimately birthed America. Can we see another Great Awakening that brings America back to its foundations? Hyatt shares what he believes the church should do in this hour in an inspiring look at how America's past could influence her future.

Jennifer LeClaire, Senior Editor, Charisma Magazine

About the Author

Dr. Eddie L. Hyatt is a seasoned minister of the Gospel with over 40 years of ministerial experience as a pastor, Bible teacher, and Professor of Theology. He holds the Doctor of Ministry from Regent University, as well as the Master of Divinity and a Master of Arts degrees from Oral Roberts University. He did post-graduate studies at the Center for Advanced Theological Studies at Fuller Theological Seminary. Dr. Hyatt has lectured on revival, Church history, and various Biblical themes in churches, conferences, and some of the major educational institutions in the world, including Christ Church Oxford University, Doulos Bible College in India, Oral Roberts University, Zion Bible College, and Christ for the Nations Institute. He has authored several books, including *2000 Years of Charismatic Christianity*, which is used as a textbook in colleges and seminaries around the world. Eddie's passion is to see God's people learn to "think Biblically" and to see authentic Spiritual awakening transform the Church and impact the world in the 21st century.

Contact Information. If you would like to correspond with Eddie for any reason, including invitations to speak, you may do so at any of the following:

Email: dreddiehyatt@gmail.com
Website: www.eddiehyatt.com
Social Media: Eddie L. Hyatt
Mailing Address: P. O. Box 3877, Grapevine TX 76099

Acknowledgments

Writing a book is never a solo achievement. That being the case with this book, I sincerely want to thank the various people who contributed to this project in various ways.

Rhonda Klug did an invaluable proof and helpful edit of the manuscript.

My wife, Dr. Susan Hyatt, contributed editorial advice, offered advice regarding the content, designed the cover, and formatted the various editions.

Other friends and family members provided prayer and financial support, without which this book could never have been written.

Finally, I want to acknowledge Almighty God, Who revealed to me in 2010 that He is not finished with America, and since that time, He has led me to resources necessary for the writing of this book.

Eddie L. Hyatt
Grapevine, Texas
June 1, 2016

Table of Contents

Preface

> To destroy a people, you must first sever their roots.
> *Alexander Solzhenitsyn*

Will America survive? The answer to that question depends on whether a nucleus of her citizens will recover and reconnect with the nation's history. A nation derives its sense of identity from its history. If you want to fundamentally change a nation, tamper with its history, for as George Orwell said in his classic, *1984*, "Whoever controls the past, controls the future." Or as Karl Marx is said to have put it, "People without a heritage are easily persuaded."[1]

This gives understanding to the statement by Barack Obama shortly after taking office, "America is not a Christian nation." This was not a statement based on the facts of history, but was, instead, a statement based on an ideology and tied to his stated goal to "fundamentally change" America. He was tampering with our history.

American history, of course, had already been tampered with before Barak Obama. Historians tamper with history, not always by changing it, but by excluding what they find objectionable. There is, for example, a noticeable void and absence when one reads modern textbook accounts of America's origins and compares that with the letters, journals and autobiographies of those same people and events. The common references

7

to faith in God, the Bible and Jesus Christ in the original accounts are glaringly missing in the modern renditions.

Modern historians seem to be embarrassed by America's overt Christian origins. They, therefore, tamper with her history by deleting or downplaying that aspect of her story. So what is being taught in public schools and universities today is a secularist revision of America's history.

The purpose of this book is not to give a detailed account of America's beginnings, but to highlight that aspect of her history that has been ignored or diminished. This is necessary, for as the Catholic scholar, Michael Novak, says, "In one key respect, the way the story of the United States has been told for the past one hundred years is wrong."[2]

What is "wrong," according to Novak, is the elimination of faith from the story of America's history. He points out that to read most historians today, one would think that America's Founders were the embodiment of "secular philosophy," when the truth is that "their faith is an *indispensable* part of their story."[3]

A unique contribution of this book is documenting how the Christianity that gave birth to America was the Christianity of the "Radical Reformers." "Radical Reformers" is a term coined by George H. Williams, the late Professor of Ecclesiastical History at Yale University, in referring to the Anabaptists, but would also include groups such as the Separatist Puritans, the English Baptists and the Quakers.[4] In some regards, it can also be a designation for Puritans in general and the early Presbyterians.

It was these "Radical Reformers" who articulated doctrines

8

of freedom of conscience, religious liberty and the freedom of the church from the state. They brought these "radical" ideals to America where they were further tried and forged in the furnace of practical experience in building a new life in the New World.

This is their story. This is America's story. This is the story of freedom-loving people everywhere.

The Original Vision

> Having undertaken for the glory of God,
> and the Advancement of the Christian Faith,
> and the Honour of our King and Country,
> a Voyage to plant the first colony
> in the northern parts of Virginia;
> [we] Do by these Presents,
> solemnly and mutually in the Presence of God
> and one another, covenant and combine
> ourselves together into a civil Body Politick
> for our better Ordering and Preservation,
> and Furtherance of the ends aforesaid.
>
> *The Mayflower Compact*

America's Christian origins are undeniable. The first act of the settlers who founded Jamestown, Virginia in 1607 was to erect a large cross they had brought from England, hold a prayer service next to it and dedicate the land of their new home to God. The Pilgrims who established the first permanent English settlement in New England in 1620 declared that they had come to this land "for the glory of God and the advancement of the Christian faith."

Eleven years later, in 1631, John Winthrop led another company of pilgrims from England and founded the city of Boston. Winthrop declared that their desire in coming to the New World was to be that "city on a hill" of which Jesus spoke and a "shining" example to the churches of Europe.

With thousands of new immigrants arriving and new towns springing up throughout New England, the New England Confederation was formed in 1643 as a representative government to arbitrate land disputes and coordinate security for the region. That they all shared a common Christian vision is evidenced in the founding Articles of Confederation, which begins with the statement,

> Whereas we all came into these parts of America with one and the same end and aim, namely to advance the kingdom of our Lord Jesus Christ and to enjoy the Liberties of the Gospel in purity with peace.[5]

This early Christian vitality waned in the late 17th and early 18th centuries, but was revitalized in what became known as "The Great Awakening." This "Great Awakening" so radically transformed colonial America that even the skeptical Benjamin Franklin referred to it as "wonderful" and said that "from being thoughtless and indifferent about religion, it seemed as if all the world were growing religious."[6] This "Great Awakening" impacted most, if not all, the Founding Fathers and had a direct bearing on the founding of the United States of America.

Reformation and religious awakenings have thus been a part of the American experience from the nation's inception. The Pilgrims, mentioned above, who settled Plymouth, Massachusetts in 1620, were Separatist

Puritans who were seeking, not only a reform of the old churches of Europe, but the formation of a new church and social order based on the New Testament. In contrast to the cold, formalized orthodoxy of the state churches of Europe, they took the New Testament as their guide and preached a personal, living faith that could be both known in the head and experienced in the heart.

Puritans Seek Reformation in England

Puritanism originally arose as a reform movement within the Church of England by those who felt that the English Church had retained too much of the old Roman Catholic order and was in further need of reform. The English reformation had begun in the 1530s largely for personal and political reasons. Henry the VIII had requested an annulment of his marriage with Catherine of Argon because she had failed to bear him a male heir to his throne.

Henry's plan was to obtain an annulment and marry Anne Boleyn. When the pope and the Roman Catholic Church refused his request, Henry was able to push the English Parliament into making him, the English monarch, the head of the English church. He was then able to move forward with his marriage to Anne Boleyn.

Because Henry had little interest in doctrinal and ecclesial reform, the Church of England differed little from the medieval Roman Catholic Church. But when Henry died in 1547 and was succeeded by the youthful Edward VI, the work of reform was greatly accelerated for Edward was favorable to the Protestant cause.

Edward, however, died in 1553 and was succeeded by his sister, Mary of Tudor, who was committed to the Roman Catholic Church. Under her reign, 288 Protestants were burned at the stake for their Protestant convictions and many fled the country and lived in exile. Protestants also persecuted Catholics when they held the reins of power.

When Mary died in 1558, she was succeeded by her sister, Elizabeth I, who was more favorable to the Protestant cause. Under Elizabeth's reign, the work of reformation was renewed in the Church of England, also known as the Anglican Church.

The Rise of Puritanism

Puritanism then arose around 1560 during the reign of Elizabeth as a sort of *avant-garde*, leading the way in the English Reformation. Their goal was to see the Church of England purged of all non-Biblical forms of worship and doctrine. Using Scripture, particularly the New Testament, as their guide, they challenged the existing church forms, rituals and structure.

Puritanism, therefore, was not a church or denomination, but a movement seeking to reform the Church of England, similar to what had happened with Martin Luther in Germany and Ulrich Zwingli in Switzerland. Their goal was not to build a new church, but to see the existing church reformed according to Scripture.

"Puritan" was not a name they chose, for they considered themselves to be Christians. It was actually put on them as an insult and slur targeting their desire for Biblical purity. William Bradford said, "And to cast contempt the more upon the sincere servants of God, they opprobriously and most injuriously gave unto and imposed upon them the name of Puritans."[7]

The movement gained great momentum in 17th century England. Its intellectual center was at Cambridge University where Puritan professors and theologians wrote and published books and tracts on religious liberty and the proper roles of the church and civil government. The movement produced such literary giants as John Milton and John Bunyan, both of whom spent time in English prisons for their faith. Puritan ideals gained the upper hand in England for a time through the revolution led by Oliver Cromwell.

It is unfortunate that modern, secular historians have sought to denigrate the Puritans by seizing upon isolated extremes that occurred at times within their ranks, and using these to try and stereotype the entire movement. For the most part they were good Christian people seeking to follow Christ at a very difficult time in history. They actually made incredible contributions to Christian history and to the founding of America, as we will see in this volume.

❧ Separatist Puritans

Because the movement challenged the hierarchical structure of the state church, Puritans came under severe persecution. This was especially true of the Separatist Puritans who left the Church of England and began forming their own illegal congregations. The Pilgrims who landed at Cape Cod in November of 1620 were part of a Separatist congregation that had experienced much persecution from the civil and religious authorities in England.

While most of the Puritans sought to reform the Church of England from within, the Separatists left the state church determining that it had become too corrupt to be reformed, primarily because of its alliance with the state. They formed their own congregations made up of voluntary members who confessed to a vital, living faith in Jesus Christ.

Since, however, the Church of England was the "official" church of the nation, these Separatist congregations were considered illegal and a threat to the peace and stability of the nation. They, therefore, came under severe persecution from both civil and ecclesiastical officials.

They were particularly despised for their rejection of the doctrines of the Divine Right of Kings and the Divine Right of the Episcopacy. These were medieval doctrines by which monarchs and church authorities wielded unmitigated authority over the masses. According to these doctrines, the monarch and/or the bishops ruled in the place of God and the people were obligated by God to obey them without question.

In their rejection of a state church, these Separatist Puritans were following in the path of those earlier continental reformers known as "Anabaptists," and in modern times known as the "Radical Reformers." Those Radical Reformers believed that Martin Luther, Ulrich Zwingli and the major Reformers had retained too much of the old Roman Catholic order, especially in their continued acceptance of a territorial church, sanctioned and upheld by the state.

Luther had struck a blow for freedom of conscience and religious liberty when at his trial for heresy he boldly resisted demands that he retract his teachings, declaring that "it is unsafe and dangerous to do anything against the conscience."[8] He went on to say, "My conscience is bound in the word of God, and I cannot and will not recant anything."[9]

Luther, however, after being condemned as a heretic, needed the protection of the powerful German Prince Frederick to keep from being arrested and executed for heresy. This dependence on the civil authority then led to Lutheranism becoming the official church of Germany. This meant that in Germany Lutheranism was upheld, and imposed on the populace, by the German princes. In England, Anglicanism was upheld and imposed by the British monarchs. Even in Calvin's city-state of Geneva there was an unhealthy intertwining of the church and civil authority. Those who dissented from the "official" form of worship and doctrine in these countries, just like in Catholic countries, were harassed, persecuted and even put to death.

The Rejection of Tyranny

Bradford, who sailed on the Mayflower and became the governor of Plymouth, tells how God revealed to them that they were not to submit to the tyrannical rule of either monarchs or bishops. He says that the Lord

16

revealed to them, not only the uselessness of high church liturgy, "but also that the lordly and tyrannous power of the prelates ought not to be submitted unto."[10]

This was revolutionary, for many thought the church could not survive without the support and protection of the state. The Separatists, however, pointed out that the church of the New Testament had flourished without the support of the state. In fact, it had flourished while often in conflict with the state, primarily because those earliest Christians had trusted in the power of the Message they preached for their success, rather than the strong arm of the civil government.

This rejection of tyrannous authority by the Separatists would become a part of the American psyche and help fuel the American Revolution and its rejection of King George and the British Parliament. This is borne out by the popular statement of the Revolution coined by Benjamin Franklin, "Rebellion to tyrants is obedience to God."

King James Persecutes the Separatists

When Elizabeth died she left no heir to the throne and so James VI of the Stuart family in Scotland was crowned James I of England in 1603. James I (who authorized the King James translation) was not friendly to the Puritan cause. He was a staunch advocate of the Divine Right of Kings and believed himself to be God's representative in the earth, head of both church and state, with absolute power over his subjects.

James, therefore, saw the Puritans, and particularly the Separatists, as a challenge to his own authority because of their opposition to the doctrines and practices of the state-controlled church. He, therefore, ordered them to conform to the Church of England, "or I will harry you out of the land."[11] One writer has said,

> The Separatists were hounded, bullied, forced to pay assessments to the Church of England, clapped into prison on trumped-up charges, and driven underground. They met in private homes, to which they came at staggered intervals and by different routes, because they were constantly being spied upon.[12]

One of the earliest Separatist congregations was formed in Scrooby, Nottinghamshire County, in 1606 with John Robinson as its pastor. A twelveqA-year-old lad, William Bradford, joined the congregation at this time. He did this, he said, in spite of the "wrath of his uncles" and the "scoff of his neighbors."[13] Bradford would later sail with members of this congregation to the New World on the Mayflower and serve as the governor of Plymouth Colony for more than thirty years.

The Move to Holland

In their precarious and dangerous situation, the members of the Scrooby congregation signed a covenant in which they committed themselves to God and to one another:

> In the fellowship of the gospel, to walk in all His ways made known unto them, according to their

best endeavors, whatsoever it should cost them, the Lord assisting them.[14]

The way they chose to walk did prove to be costly, and because of the persecution, they began to discuss moving as a congregation to Holland, as they had heard there was religious freedom there. However, even their attempts to depart their beloved homeland were opposed by British authorities who arrested several of their number when they discovered their plans to leave the country.

In one final attempt to get away to Holland, they hired the services of a Dutch ship and sea captain and made plans to leave in secret. The men decided to travel by land with their belongings to the place of departure and the women and children would travel by boat and meet with them at the ship that would take them to Holland.

During their trip along the coast, some of the women became very sick and asked the seamen to pull into shore and allow them to rest momentarily on land. In the meantime, their husbands reached the ship and went aboard where they stowed their belongings and then watched for their wives and children to arrive.

Suddenly the Dutch sea captain spied a company of armed men coming toward them. Fearing arrest and the confiscation of his ship, he quickly raised anchor, hoisted the sails, and sailed away. The men were frantic and pleaded with him to wait for their wives and children. He refused, however, and sailed away to Holland while the men with heavy hearts watched the shores of England disappear along with their wives and children.

In the meantime, the women and children arrived in time to see their husbands and fathers sailing away and disappearing in the distance. One can only imagine the depth of distress and anguish that must have filled their hearts.

The company of armed men arrived, arrested the women and marched them with their children back into the city. The authorities, however, did not know what to do with them, for they were crying in distress while their small children clung to them, crying and quaking from the cold.

They were hurried from one court and justice to another who knew not what to do with them, for they were penniless and homeless, having sold everything for the move to Holland. Finally, growing weary and not knowing what to do with them, the authorities dropped all charges and let them go free.

Although it was a distressing time, it brought public attention to the Separatist cause and prompted much compassion from those who observed the women and their children in such distress. In the midst of these trials they found solace in their faith and in prayer, and their godly behavior left a deep impression on the minds of many and caused many to look into the Separatist cause.

Bradford says that in spite of "all these storms of opposition," they all finally got over to Holland, "some at one time and some at another."[15] They were finally all reunited in Amsterdam where they spent about one year and then moved to the city of Leyden. At this time, they were about 125 in number.

Life in Holland and
The Vision for a New Home

The Puritans in general, and the Leyden congregation in particular, had a vision to recover the purity and pattern of the New Testament church, which they referred to as the "primitive church." In his memoirs, written later in life, Bradford spoke of the "fervent zeal" and "humble love" of the Leyden congregation and said, "They came as near the primitive pattern of the first churches as any other church of these latter times have done."[16]

Even before leaving England, they developed principles of self-government that would serve them well in the New World. In Holland they lived in close community, but they did not live communally. Although they shared with one another and bore one another's burdens as commanded in Scripture, they practiced private ownership of property and believed it to be the Biblical approach.

In his memoirs, Bradford quotes the second Decalogue of the Ten Commandments in this regard, which forbids the coveting of that which belongs to another. They saw this as a Biblical affirmation of individual and private ownership of property.

Their pastor, John Robinson, was a strong, compassionate leader. A graduate of Cambridge University, he left the Church of England to join the Separatists and suffer with them because he believed theirs to be a righteous cause. Bradford says there was such a mutual love and respect between him and the people that it was hard to judge "whether he delighted more in having such a people, or they in having such a pastor."[17]

Their love for one another and their vision for a restoration of New Testament Christianity attracted others to them. Whereas approximately 125 initially settled in Leyden, their numbers in Leyden grew to around five hundred, with many coming from England to be a part of their community and share in their vision.

Although they had religious liberty in Holland, they were treated as second-class citizens and permitted only to engage in menial labor and paid wages on which they could barely subsist. They generally bore these difficulties with courage and cheerfulness, but they quickly aged and a number were "taken away by death."[18] What was even more difficult to bear was that many of their children were being led astray by undesirable influences in the Dutch culture.

Although all of these things factored into their decision to seek a new home in the New World, they were moved primarily by their faith and their desire to be instruments for taking the Gospel to those who had never heard the Good News. Concerning this missionary vision, Bradford wrote,

Lastly (and which was not least), a great hope and inward zeal they had of laying some good foundation, or at least to make some way thereunto, for the propagating and advancing of the gospel of the kingdom of Christ in those remote parts of the world; yea though they should be but even as stepping-stones unto others for the performing of so great a work.[19]

So, they began searching for a place more suitable to their vision and more compatible with their English culture. In their search, they were put in contact with a group of English businessmen whom William Bradford called "Adventurers," and would be known today as "venture capitalists." These "Adventurers" agreed to underwrite the rental of a ship and provisions to take them to the New World, and in return the Pilgrims would pay them back with interest.

Although the entire congregation would have liked to have moved together, it became obvious that a small portion of the congregation would have to go first and the rest follow at a later time.

After much wrangling and questioning by government officials, they were finally granted a patent by English officials authorizing them to settle in Northern Virginia. A day was then set aside for departure in a ship, the Speedwell, which would take them to England where they would rendezvous with another ship, the Mayflower, and the two ships would carry them to the New World.

The Journey Begins in Prayer

With these important issues in place, the Pilgrims, set aside "a day of solemn humiliation" to seek the Lord's blessing and guidance before the departure on July 22, 1620. They began the day with Robinson exhorting them from Ezra 8:21, which reads, *And there by the river I proclaimed a fast that we might humble ourselves before our God* and *seek of him a right way for us . . . ..* After Robinson's exhortation, Bradford says, "The rest of the time was spent in pouring our prayers to the Lord with great fervency, mixed with abundance of tears."[20]

The time of departure came and they all boarded the ship where they exchanged their final goodbyes and prayed together one final time. It was a very moving and emotional scene with many sighs and tears, for they realized that it could be the last time they would see family and friends.

The time came for the ship to sail and those who were remaining behind were notified that they must disembark. But before returning to shore, they had one final prayer. Bradford says,

> Their reverend pastor falling down on his knees (and they all with him) with watery cheeks commended them with most fervent prayers to the Lord and his blessing. And then with mutual embraces and many tears they took their leaves one of another, which proved to be the last leave to many of them.[21]

They Become "Pilgrims"

It was from this beginning of their epic journey that this congregation was given the name "Pilgrims," which is the only name by which they are now known. The name was given to them by Bradford in his account of their departure to the New World. He wrote,

24

So they left that goodly and pleasant city which had been their resting place near twelve years; but they knew they were *pilgrims*, and looked not much on these things, but lifted up their eyes to the heavens, their dearest country, and quieted their spirits.[22]

From Delftshaven they sailed to Southampton, England, and after many more trials, including the discovery that the Speedwell was not seaworthy, they finally sailed on the Mayflower from Plymouth, England, on September 6, 1620, with 102 passengers and around thirty crew members.

Among their number were several individuals who were not part of the Leyden congregation but had been recruited by the Adventurers, who although in verbal agreement with the vision of the Pilgrims, were also motivated by monetary profit. In his account, Bradford refers to them as "strangers" and they proved to be problematic for the entire venture since they did not share the vision and values of the Pilgrims.

The Pilgrims Find a New Home in America

Although they were planning to settle in Northern Virginia, the Mayflower was blown off course and they finally landed at Cape Cod in present day Massachusetts in early November after sixty-five days at sea. It was a daunting, chilling experience as they looked out on the cold, dark terrain with no warm homes or friends waiting to welcome them.

When the "strangers" on board began to complain and talk of mutiny, the Pilgrims became the stabilizing force.

They drew up a "compact," patterned after the Puritan church covenants, for all adult males to sign. In this covenant, or compact, those who signed agreed to live in peace with one another and obey the laws that would from time to time be instituted for the good of the community.

This document is known as the Mayflower Compact and it reads, in part,

> In the name of God, Amen! Having undertaken for the glory of God, and the Advancement of the Christian Faith, and the Honour of our King and Country, a Voyage to plant the first colony in the northern parts of Virginia; [we] Do by these Presents, solemnly and mutually in the Presence of God and one another, covenant and combine ourselves together into a civil Body Politick for our better Ordering and Preservation, and Furtherance of the ends aforesaid.

This Compact is considered by many to be a forerunner of America's founding documents. Indeed, they realized that they were more than a church; they were now a "civil body politic," and they agreed to live by laws that their elected leaders would implement.

After signing the Mayflower Compact, the passengers disembarked and stepped onto the sands of Cape Cod near present day Provincetown. Bradford (1590-1657), who would soon thereafter become governor of the colony, described their actions upon stepping ashore in the New World. He wrote,

Being thus arrived in a good harbor and brought safe to land, they fell upon their knees and blessed the God of heaven, who had brought them over the vast and furious ocean, and delivered them from all the perils and miseries thereof. They had begun their long journey by kneeling on the dock at Delftshaven to ask God's blessing; they ended it on the sands of Cape Cod, kneeling to thank Him for that blessing.[23]

ॐॐ Chapter 2 ॐॐ

Implementing the Vision

> They were equal to any standard of excellence
> known to history. Their range was narrow,
> but in it they were supreme.
>
> *Samuel Eliot Morrison, Historian*

Although relieved to have reached their destination, the Pilgrims would face unimaginable challenges ahead. It was winter in New England, and they had to find a suitable location in which to settle. The land would have to be cleared and suitable housing built. Meantime, the captain of the Mayflower was anxious to return to England, so they would have to move quickly.

After the signing of the Mayflower Compact, they chose John Carver to be their governor. Four months later, Carver died after coming in from the field complaining of intense pain in his head. In his place, they chose William Bradford (1590-1657), and Governor Bradford served in this capacity for over thirty years.

William Brewster, who was a teaching elder in the Leyden congregation, was looked upon as the spiritual leader. Myles Standish, a thirty-eight-year-old soldier of fortune, was recruited by the Adventurers to accompany the Pilgrims and provide security and military advice where needed. Although originally one of the "strangers," Standish identified with the Pilgrims and became one of the most respected leaders of the Plymouth Plantation.

Finding a Place of Habitation

Realizing that Cape Cod was not a suitable place for them to settle, they spent several weeks exploring along the coast and seeking to make contact with any natives of the area. Finally, in mid-December, they found a harbor fit for shipping, while on the land, they found several running brooks and a hill overlooking the harbor from which they could easily defend the area.

They discovered that the name of the harbor was "Plymouth," so named by the English explorer, John Smith, a few years prior to their arrival. It must have seemed Providential, for as a result of a number of unforeseen incidents before departing England, they had finally sailed from "Plymouth."

A Bitter First Winter

As they worked in the bitter cold at clearing the land and building simple houses in which to live, many became deathly sick. The austere conditions and lack of proper nourishment were overwhelming. Those who were able did their best to care for those who were sick. But in spite of their best efforts, almost half of their number died that first winter.

Bradford himself was confined to bed for an extended period of time and his wife died even before they had disembarked from the Mayflower. There were many sad hearts that first winter as they buried their loved ones beneath the frozen New England sod.

In spite of the hardships, they never stopped praying, hoping and trusting. And with the spring thaw came two English speaking Native Americans whom the Pilgrims believed were providentially sent by God in answer to their prayers. Samoset came first, and then he introduced them to Squanto.

Indian Relations

Squanto, whom Bradford called "a special instrument sent from God for their good," instructed the Pilgrims in farming, hunting and fishing. This was life-saving, for in England they had been craftsmen and townspeople and without these new skills, they would not have survived in the wilderness of New England.

Squanto also arranged a special meeting between Bradford and Massasoit, who was Chief of the Wampanoag, the most powerful tribe in the region. Massasoit arrived at the plantation with sixty of his warriors, and the Pilgrims received him with the respect they would have shown a dignitary in England. They ushered him to a building where they seated him on a special green rug with three or four cushions. Bradford then arrived and after exchanging cordial greetings, they had a drink together and discussed the need for friendly and mutual relations.

Bradford and Massasoit agreed on a peace treaty, promising mutual friendship and security. According to Bradford, it included the following:

1. That neither Massasoit nor any of his people would do harm to any of their people.

2. That if any Wampanoag took away anything from the Pilgrims, Massasoit would cause it to be restored, and they would do likewise.

3. That they would aid one another in the event of an outside attack on either.

This first American security pact opened the way for trade and free movement between the Wampanoag and the Pilgrims. Within a year, the Pilgrims had signed similar peace treaties with several other tribes. Meantime, the treaty with the Wampanoag was kept faithfully for over fifty years, until Massasoit's son, Metacom, became Chief. He was better known in history by his chosen name, "King Philip."

After the treaty was signed, Massasoit returned to his place called Sowams, which was located about forty miles from Plymouth in what would be present day Barrington, Rhode Island. Squanto, however, remained with the Pilgrims as did Samoset, Hobomok, and possibly other natives. Their assistance to the Pilgrims was invaluable, serving them as guides and interpreters, and showing them how to farm, fish and hunt.

Indeed, the first generation of immigrants to New England treated the natives with what Dr. Samuel Eliot Morison called "a combination of justice, wisdom and mercy."[24] Examples of this are found in the account of the unnamed Pilgrim in *Mourt's Relations*, which is actually a collection of several Pilgrim journals first published in 1622.

The unnamed Pilgrim tells of Squanto leading several of their number to the Massachusetts tribe and acting as their interpreter. The Pilgrims wanted to trade with them, especially for furs. There was a great market for beaver fur back in England and they saw this as a way to pay off their debt to the Adventurers. They also saw it as a way to establish friendly relations with the natives, whom they hoped to reach with the Gospel of Jesus Christ.

In their journey, they came across a group of women working with corn and wearing beaver coats. Squanto, the writer says, wanted to "rifle" the women and take their furs. "They are a bad people and have oft threatened you," he said. The Pilgrims replied, "Were they ever so bad, we would not wrong them, or give them any just occasion against us."[25]

They insisted that the women be offered a fair price for their furs, and Squanto complied. The women agreed to the price, removed their beaver coats, and then wrapped themselves in foliage.

Obviously relieved and impressed at how they were treated, the women accompanied the Pilgrims back to their boat. In regards to the women being careful to cover themselves, the writer further commented, "Indeed, they are more modest than some of our English women."[26]

The First Thanksgiving

As the Pilgrims completed the final gathering of their crops that first fall in the New World, there was a sense of thankfulness in many hearts. Just a few months prior, they had been living on the edge of starvation and wondering if they would survive. Now they had plenty.

Not only did they have an abundance of food, but now they also had peace with their neighbors. In fact, one unnamed Pilgrim wrote back to England,

> We have found the Indians very faithful in their covenant of peace with us, very loving and ready to pleasure us. We often go to them, and they come to us. And we, for our parts, walk as peaceably and safely in the wood as in the highways of England.[27]

Governor Bradford, therefore, declared a certain day to be set aside as a day of thanksgiving in which to "rejoice together after we had gathered the fruit of our labors."[28] Word of the event soon spread and many of their Native American friends arrived to participate in the celebration.

Massasoit himself arrived with ninety of his people to participate in the festivities. It soon became obvious that they would need more food, so Massasoit and his men went out and killed five deer and dressed them for the feast.

One can only imagine the emotions that filled their hearts as, in the presence of their new Native American friends, they joined Elder William Brewster in lifting up their hearts in praise and thanksgiving to God.

The Pilgrims did not seek to force their faith on the Indians, but neither did they hide their faith. After all, in the Mayflower Compact they had clearly stated that they had come to the New World for the glory of God and the advancement of the Christian faith.

The day turned out to be more than they could have imagined. Not only did they enjoy meals together with thankful hearts, but they also engaged in shooting matches and other friendly forms of competition. It was such an enjoyable time that the one Day of Thanksgiving was extended for three full days.

And yes, it is almost certain that there was turkey at the first Thanksgiving for Governor Bradford had sent out four men to hunt for "fowl" who returned with enough "fowl" to last them an entire week.[29]

A Remarkable Answer to Prayer

The next recorded Thanksgiving Day among the Pilgrims was celebrated in the fall of 1623, after a remarkable answer to prayer that saved their harvests, and, probably, their lives. Bradford tells how the summer of 1623 was unusually hot with no rain whatsoever. As the blazing sun beat down day after day the land became parched and the corn, their primary staple, began to dry up along with other vegetables they had planted. Alone in the New England wilderness, it looked as though hunger would be their lot in the days ahead, and maybe starvation. It was a very critical moment in time.

Facing such drought and bleak conditions, Bradford

called the Plymouth community to a day of "humiliation and prayer."[30] By "humiliation" he did not mean a groveling or self-flagellation, but recognition of and repentance for the human tendency to trust in one's own human strength and ability, rather than in God.

Their day of humiliation and prayer began like the many preceding days, very hot, with not a single cloud in the sky. But before the day was over, God gave them, Bradford said, "a gracious and speedy answer, both to their own and the Indians' admiration that lived amongst them." Bradford goes on to say,

> For all the morning and the greatest part of the day, it was clear weather and very hot, and not a cloud or any sign of rain to be seen; yet toward evening it began to overcast, and shortly after to rain with such sweet and gentle showers as gave them cause of rejoicing and blessing God. It came without wind or thunder or any violence, and by degrees in that abundance as that the earth was thoroughly wet and soaked . . . which did so apparently revive and quicken the decayed corn and other fruits as was wonderful to see, and made the Indians astonished to behold. And afterwards the Lord sent them such seasonable showers, with interchange of fair weather as, through His blessing, caused a fruitful and liberal harvest, to their no small comfort and rejoicing. For which mercy, in time convenient, they also set apart *a day of thanksgiving.*[31]

The Pilgrims' habit of setting aside special days for

prayer, fasting, and thanksgiving became a part of the cultural experience of New England and was practiced by succeeding generations. From there, it found its way into the American culture where their influence in this regard may still be seen.

Their Failed Experiment with Socialism

The "Adventurers"—those who funded the Pilgrims' journey to America—required that they live communally for seven years with everyone receiving the same recompense for their work. This meant that there was no private ownership; instead, everyone worked fields owned by the plantation. The harvest went into a common fund from which each family received a portion for their sustenance. The remainder was used to pay their debt.

The same was true of fishing and furs obtained by trading. No one was rewarded for their individual labor. Everyone received an equal amount for their basic necessities and the rest went into the common fund. The agreement was that at the end of seven years, assuming all debts were cleared, anything left in the common fund would be divided among the Pilgrim families.

Bradford, who served as Governor of Plymouth for over thirty years, told of the challenges of this socialist system. Young men, he said, resented getting paid the same as older men when they did so much more of the work. As a result, they tended to slouch and give only a half-hearted effort since they knew they would receive the same, no matter how hard they worked.

The older men felt they deserved more honor and recompense because of their age and resented getting paid the same as the youngsters in their midst. Bradford said that the women often refused to go to the fields to work, complaining of headaches, and to have compelled them to go would have been considered tyranny and oppression.

This socialist system discouraged work and innovation and almost destroyed the colony. When it became obvious that lack and, perhaps, starvation would be their lot, Bradford and the leaders of the colony decided to make a change. After much prayer and discussion, they decided to dispense with that part of the agreement that required them to live communally and to replace it with a free enterprise system.

They Experience the Gain of Free Enterprise

According to Bradford, they then divided the land around them, allotting to each family a certain portion that would be theirs to work and use for their own needs. Bradford said there was an immediate change. The young men began to work much harder because they knew they would enjoy the fruit of their own labors. There were no more complaints from the older men for the same reason. And now the women were seen going into the fields to work, taking the children with them, because they knew that they and their families would benefit personally.

Instead of lacking food, each family now grew more food and corn than they needed, and they began to trade with one another for furnishings, clothes, and other goods. They also had enough excess to trade with the Indians for furs and other items. In short, the colony began to prosper when it got rid of its socialist form of government and implemented a free, entrepreneurial system. Of their experience with socialism, Bradford wrote,

> This community [socialism] was found to breed much confusion and discontent and retard much employment that would have been to their benefit and comfort . . . and showed the vanity of that conceit of Plato's, and applauded by some of later times, that the taking away of property and bringing in community into a commonwealth would make them happy and flourishing; as if they were wiser than God.[32]

From then on, the Plymouth colony practiced private ownership of property and free enterprise. Also, taking the Separatist/Congregational form of church government as their model, they decentralized authority and the people chose their leaders. Elections were held annually for governor and for seven council members who assisted and advised the governor. They also had a written constitution by which they agreed to live, which we know as the Mayflower Compact. Historian, Benjamin Hart, says,

> What Abraham Lincoln described as government "of the people, by the people and for the people," was inherited from a tradition beginning with the Congregationalist Protestant settlement in Plymouth, Massachusetts, in the 1620s.[33]

The Vision Expands

Whereas we all came into these parts of America
with one and the same end and aim,
namely to advance the kingdom
of our Lord Jesus Christ
and enjoy the Liberties of the Gospel
in purity and peace.

Constitution of the New England Confederation, 1643

During the ensuing years, a few more Separatists migrated to New England, but their numbers remained small until a new wave of persecution was launched against all Puritans by Charles I, beginning around 1628. This resulted in a massive wave of Puritan immigration to New England.

Persecution Because of Their Faith

Shortly after assuming the English throne on March 27, 1625, Charles I married the French Catholic, Henrietta Maria, which raised suspicions and fears among the Protestant groups of England. Their concerns were heightened when Charles installed the high church, anti-

Puritan, William Laud, as Archbishop of Canterbury. Laud proceeded to create a list, which he gave to the king, of English clergymen with either an "O" or a "P" in front of their name. Those with an "O" were identified as orthodox and worthy of the Crown's favor. Those marked with a "P" were identified as Puritan and were to be targeted for persecution, with the goal of forcing them to conform.

A new wave of persecution thus erupted, with Puritans being forced from their pastorates, harassed, and imprisoned. Most had held out a hope of the Church of England being reformed, but they now saw those hopes dashed under the onslaught of this new persecution. As a result, shiploads of religious refugees began departing England for the shores of New England. Between 1630 and 1640, over twenty thousand Puritans migrated to New England.

At times, it must have seemed that all of England was leaving, including some of the brightest theologians and preachers in all of England. Most were not Separatists, but they now had a new appreciation for the Separatists and their decision to begin anew and seek to build a Christian community from the ground up. One of the earliest groups in this new wave of immigrants was led by John Winthrop.

John Winthrop
and the Founding of Massachusetts

John Winthrop (1588-1649) was born into a wealthy English family and had yearnings towards God from the time of his youth. He was very intelligent and entered

Cambridge at the age of sixteen and became a Justice of the Peace at the age of eighteen. He obviously had a bright future in law and as an English jurist.

At Cambridge, however, he was exposed to the Puritan way and was attracted to the Reformed way of thinking about God, government, and church. He attended church regularly and was faithful to pray and read his Bible, but he continued to struggle in his soul. He wrote,

> So I waxed exceedingly discontent and impatient, being sometimes ready to fret and storm against God, because I found not that blessing upon my prayers and other means that I did expect.[34]

The change came when he read a book by William Perkins, a Puritan writer, who pointed out that pagans with their commitment to religious rituals are as deserving of salvation as Christians who trust in their rituals. That word pierced his heart and he suddenly saw himself as a "hypocrite," trusting in his own works for salvation. He wrote, "I acknowledged my unfaithfulness and pride of heart, and turned to my God."[35]

Winthrop suddenly saw that he had no virtue in himself and only Christ—Christ alone—could save him from his sins. He experienced a "new birth" and realized that his judicial career in English law was in conflict with the call of God on his life. He later wrote, "I found that the world had stolen away my love for God."[36]

Winthrop became the leader of a group of Puritans that met at Cambridge on a regular basis. With the new persecution raising its ugly head, they discussed the possibility of settling in the New World, especially since the Pilgrims had shown that it could be done. In their discussions, they saw the possibility that in the New World, removed from the continual harassment of the state and the state-run church, they could exhibit a model of New Testament Christianity for the rest of the world to see.

At one of their conferences, Winthrop and a number of Puritan businessmen decided to assume control of the Massachusetts Bay Company, which possessed a government charter for a settlement in New England. They asked and received permission to carry the charter with them to New England.

Taking the charter with them was significant, for it meant that the required periodic meetings of the officers would take place in the New World. This was a stroke of genius, for it served to sever them from the influence of the English church and state, and it allowed them to apply and develop their ideals of self-government.

The necessary preparations were made and a flotilla of eleven ships, led by the *Arbella*, and carrying over seven hundred passengers, departed for the New World on February 30, 1630.

During the journey across the Atlantic, Winthrop preached a sermon entitled "A Model of Christian Charity." In it he exhorted his fellow pilgrims that "the eyes of the world are upon us" and that God would have them, in their new home, to be that "city on a hill" of which Jesus spoke, a shining light exhibiting a model of Christian living for the rest of mankind to see.

The flotilla landed at Salem, but Winthrop and his company moved to Shawmut Peninsula where they founded what is now the city of Boston. As a result of their clearly stated vision and the persecution back in England, Puritans began pouring into the Massachusetts Bay Colony. Included in this number were some of the best minds and most powerful preachers in England, leading Hart to comment,

> Distinguished graduates from Cambridge and Oxford, "silenced" by Laud, poured into the colony, and many brought whole congregations with them. The houses of worship they built were bleak. There was no organ music, no stained glass windows and no heating. The benches they sat on were hard. But nowhere in the world was the Gospel expounded more Masterfully from the pulpit.[37]

Although the new immigrants were not all Separatists, like their neighbors in Plymouth, they shared with Plymouth the vision for a complete reformation of Christendom, and they worked hard to create a church and Christian society based on their understanding of the Bible, particularly the New Testament. This led the late Harvard professor, Perry Miller, to describe this Puritan migration as,

> An organized task force of Christians, executing a flank attack on the corruptions of Christendom. These Puritans did not flee to America; they went in order to work out the complete reformation which was not yet accomplished in England and Europe, but which they believed would quickly be

accomplished back there if only the saints had a working model to guide them.[38]

Developing a New Church Model

Back in England, most of these new immigrants had worked within the Anglican Church for reform. Now that they were removed to the New World, many questions were posed to their minds. How much of the Anglican Church model should they retain? How much of the Separatist model should they adopt? What did the New Testament have to say concerning these matters?

Before departing England, Winslow, in spite of the persecution, expressed a desire to maintain friendly ties with the mother church. In a document called "A Humble Request," Winslow and others asked to be remembered by those in the homeland and described themselves as "those who esteem it our honor to call the Church of England from whence we rise, our dear mother."[39]

After arriving in New England, however, they sought to establish friendly relations with the Separatists at Plymouth and showed an immediate interest in that church's organization. Winthrop, in fact, expressed his desire that the Plymouth Church will "not be wanting in helping them" toward their necessary church organization.[40] At this early date, in their new environment, they were obviously moving carefully and prudently in implementing the reforms they had so long desired and discussed in the Old World.

They eventually dispensed with the episcopal/Anglican

form of church government, with its hierarchy and ruling bishops. In its place they adopted a congregational model more in line with the Separatists in Plymouth. They also banished all hereditary privilege, moving towards a classless society in which social rank was unimportant. If social rank was unimportant to Jesus, they reasoned, why should it be important to them? Being separated from the homeland by an ocean, they were able to make these changes without "formally" severing ties with the Church of England.

The congregational model meant that each congregation was autonomous and self-governing. It also meant that members of a local congregation were involved in choosing their leaders. Synods or summits of leaders from the various congregations would meet on a regular basis to discuss issues that concerned them all. These synods, however, held no power over the local congregations, but could only counsel and advise.

Here we see the seeds of a federalist system; that is, a loose confederation of many smaller and local governments or communities, all retaining their local autonomy. This, they believed, was how the church of the New Testament functioned.

The Relationship of Church and State

The development of the Puritan church model had a bearing on how they developed their civil government. Decentralized authority with power centered in the people was an important ideal in this regard. Regular elections were held with civil officials chosen by the voters. These developments were important steps leading to the founding principles of the United States. Hart is thus correct in saying,

> The movement toward democracy in Massachusetts had nothing to do with following a liberal or "Enlightenment" political philosophy. Rather, it was a natural by-product of the Puritans making a conscious attempt to build a commonwealth within God's precepts. Christian and democratic institutions are compatible. Thus, we begin to see how American ways of government and American political thought can be traced directly to the religious and political institutions of New England.[41]

Seeking to preserve the purity of the church, ministers were not allowed to hold civil office. This "separation" shows their move toward the views of the Radical Reformers who emphasized how the church had become corrupt when Constantine merged it with the state. Civil concerns, they concluded, could cause pastors and ministers to lose their focus and expose them to temptations that would be detrimental to their highest calling.

That this separation was unidirectional, to protect the church from the government, is shown in the establishment of the "Election Sermon" in 1633. Each year at the time of the annual election of the governor and his assistants, a minister was appointed to preach an "Election Sermon." This was a major event, attended by both religious and civil leaders. After the delivery of the sermon, it was then printed and distributed throughout the colony. In 1860, John Wingate Thornton wrote,

> The annual "Election Sermon" — a perpetual memorial, continued down through the generations from century to century — still bears witness that our fathers ever began their civil year and its responsibilities with an appeal to Heaven, and recognized Christian morality as the only basis of good laws.[42]

The Puritan Vision

The Puritan vision was a Christian commonwealth in which godly pastors exerted their influence, not only in the church, but in the public and civic realm, as well. Church attendance was open to all, but only those who could testify of a personal, saving relationship with Jesus Christ could be members. Only church members could vote in civic elections and civic leaders were expected to be Christians who would consult with pastors concerning political and civic issues.

What, therefore, the Puritans implemented in America was not a theocracy, but neither was there any thought of a separation of the church from the state, such as is touted today. They believed that God had created society as a unified whole to reflect His glory. Church and state, the individual and the public, were all related spheres and all were to function under the Lordship of Christ, whose government was to be administered through godly civic leaders with the help of pastors and ministers.

These Puritans held out a hope that, in the wilderness of New England, they would demonstrate what could happen if a body of Christians were allowed to live their lives wholly to God. Mark Noll, Professor of Church History at Wheaton College, says the Puritan mission to America was "both to restore the purity of early Christianity and to be a "city on the hill" for those who remained in Europe"[43]

From Church Covenant to Constitution

From the very beginning the Puritan immigrants to America drew up written statements that defined the purpose of their communities and the basis on which they would function. These covenants, or compacts, were modeled after the church covenants that had been part of the Separatist churches in England.

These statements always gave recognition to God and prioritized the Gospel of Jesus Christ as the reason for their existence. For example, the 1639 founding document of Connecticut entitled "The Fundamental Orders of Connecticut," states,

> We, the inhabitants and residents of Windsor, Hartford, and Wethersfield, knowing where a people are gathered together the word of God requires that to maintain the peace and union of such a people there ought to be an orderly and decent government established according to God . . . we do for ourselves and our successors enter into combination and confederation together, to maintain and preserve the liberty and purity of the

Gospel of our Lord Jesus Christ, which we now profess."[44]

The Puritans saw these written statements as social compacts, not only between themselves, but also between their society and God. They believed that if they kept their part of the agreement and walked uprightly before the Lord, their communities would be blessed. On the other hand, disobedience to God's commands, even by some in their midst, could bring judgment for the entire community. For this reason, they tended to hold one another accountable. It is also the reason that laws were passed outlawing adultery, fornication, profanity, drunkenness and Sabbath breaking.

These covenants meant that those who became a part of these communities were agreeing to be ruled, not by a monarch, but by laws to which they all agreed. In this, they were functioning more as a "republic" than as a pure democracy. The primary difference between a republic and a democracy is that a republic has a constitution or bill of rights guaranteeing certain rights to all citizens. In both, governmental authority rests with the people, but in a republic that authority is curtailed by the written constitution for the purpose of protecting minorities from the tyranny of a majority.

There is no question that these early covenants were precursors to the founding documents of the United States of America. Gary Amos and Richard Gardiner are correct to say, "The early New England constitutions were covenants. These covenants clearly foreshadowed the United States Constitution."[45]

Because of the nature of these covenants, they were considered to be sacred oaths between the society and Almighty God. This covenantal attitude became a part of the psyche of colonial America and was present at the institution of America's founding documents. This is why Hart says,

> The U.S. Constitution has worked because there has been a sacred aura surrounding the document; it has been something more than a legal contract; it was a covenant, an oath before God, very much related to the covenant the Pilgrims signed. Indeed, when the President takes his oath of office he places his hand on a Bible and swears before Almighty God to uphold the Constitution of the United States. He makes a sacred promise; and the same holds true for Supreme Court justices who take an oath to follow the letter of the written Constitution. The moment America's leaders begin treating the Constitution as though it were a mere sheet of paper is the moment the American Republic—or American Covenant—ends.[46]

The Puritan Emphasis on Education

Among those early Puritan immigrants to America, at least one hundred had received theological training at Cambridge University, which was a center of Puritan reform. At least thirty had received theological training at Oxford. It is, therefore, no surprise that, early on, there was a desire for an educational system that would prepare pastors for the churches and perpetuate the Puritan vision of Christian reform.

As a result, Harvard College, now Harvard University, was formed in 1636 to train ministers and pastors for the Puritan churches. Harvard was thoroughly Christian and its founding mission statement included the following statement,

> Let every student be plainly instructed and earnestly pressed that the main end of life and study is to know God and His Son Jesus Christ, which is eternal life, John 17:3, and therefore to lay Christ in the bottom as the only foundation of all knowledge and learning.[47]

In 1701, Puritans in Connecticut opened Yale College, now Yale University, to give the youth a "liberal and religious education so that leaders for the churches should not be lacking."[48] In fact, all the early colleges in America were founded to train ministers and to propagate the rediscovered Christian message of the Reformers. And these are the colleges in which America's Founders received their training.

Lower levels of education were also important. In 1642, the Massachusetts legislature threatened town leaders with fines if they did not see that all children were "trained to read and understand the principles of religion." Five years later, a law was passed requiring each town of at least fifty households to appoint a teacher for training the youth. Professor Mark Noll points out that this attention to learning "made New England one of the world's most literate places by the end of the century."[49] Until after the Civil War, most educational programs in the United States, from grade schools through universities, were modeled on patterns established by those first Puritan settlers.[50]

Education was important for these early immigrants and for the Founders because, in a democracy or republic, only an educated and informed populace could choose wise leaders and not be taken in by charlatans. This is why David Ramsey, in *History of the United States*, published in 1816, declared that America's Founders, "Wisely judged learning and religion to be the firmest pillars of the church and commonwealth."

The United Colonies of New England

In 1643 the colonies of Plymouth, Massachusetts, Connecticut, and New Haven formed a confederation, which they called "The New England Confederation," but also referred to in their constitution as "The United Colonies of New England." With new towns and colonies springing up and disputes over boundaries arising, it was obvious that a common government and jurisdiction was needed. There was also the felt need that they not become isolated from one another, especially since some of the Indian tribes had shown signs of hostility.

Dated May 19, 1643, the opening statement of the constitution for this confederation expressly declares why they had all come to the New World. It reads,

Whereas we all came into these parts of America

with one and the same end and aim, namely to advance the kingdom of our Lord Jesus Christ and enjoy the Liberties of the Gospel in purity and peace.[51]

The constitution provided that each colony would choose two representatives who would form a council of eight. This council of eight was invested with power to arbitrate boundary disputes, coordinate mutual defense, and facilitate mutual advice and support. It was clearly stated that this council was also brought into existence for "preserving and propagating the truth and liberties of the Gospel."[52]

The constitution also provided that the eight council members would choose one of their number as president "whose office and work shall be to take care and direct for a comely carrying on of all proceedings."[53] They were careful to state that this office of president was not invested with any executive power "by which he shall hinder the propounding or progress of any business, or in any way cast the scales otherwise than in the precedent Article is agreed."[54]

There is no question that this federalist system, in which each individual colony retained its autonomy, and the powers of government were limited by the constitution, was a forerunner of the federalist system that would be created at Philadelphia in 1776 and 1787. The United Colonies of New England clearly foreshadowed the United States of America in both its form of government and in its Christian character.

Radical Reformers

There is one great God and power
that has made the world and all things therein,
to whom you and I and all people owe their being
and well-being, and to whom you and I must
one day give an account for all
that we do in this world.

William Penn, Founder of Pennsylvania

Although the record of the Puritans of New England has dominated the perceptions of America's history, and for good reason, Christianity preceded them to the New World through French and Spanish Catholic missionaries who shared their faith with the natives, often at great sacrifice, including their own lives. The Puritans were also preceded by those who established the first permanent English settlement in the New World at Jamestown, Virginia, in 1607.

Early Spanish Missionaries

The Spanish missionaries experienced great success, particularly in the southeast and southwest, establishing missions and seeking to minister to the practical needs of the natives. For example, by 1630 the Spanish-Catholic missionary responsible for an area that encompasses present day New Mexico, Alonso de Benavides, reported that eighty thousand Native Americans had been baptized.[55]

Although they helped to bring Christianity to the American continent and are to be commended for their zeal and sacrifice, these Catholic missionaries did not have the vision or the theological framework for establishing a new nation rooted in religious liberty. The Catholic, Anglican, and Lutheran churches of Europe all held to the medieval idea of a territorial church that is supported and sanctioned by the state.

These state churches of Europe and England used the strong arm of the state to enforce their doctrine and polity. Dissenters were harassed, imprisoned, and even put to death. It was left to the more radical groups of the Reformation—the Separatist Puritans, Baptists and Quakers—to develop concepts of religious liberty and freedom of conscience that have become hallmarks of Western civilization.

Jamestown and Virginia

Like the earlier Spanish missionaries, the earlier settlement of 1607 in Jamestown, Virginia, being Anglican, did not have the advantage of the theological framework of the Radical Reformers. Neither were there any women or children on that initial voyage, a clear indication that they did not have the same vision for establishing community and society as did the immigrants to New England.

Nonetheless, they saw their mission to the New World within a Christian context. This was made clear when their chaplain, Rev. Robert Hunt, designated a three-day period of prayer and repentance before disembarking. Much bickering and dissension had erupted during the voyage and Hunt believed that if they were to successfully consecrate the land for God's purposes, there must be repentance and a contrition of heart.

After the three days of prayer, Hunt led the party to the wind-swept shore of Cape Henry where they erected a seven-foot oak cross, brought from England. They then gathered around the cross, holding the first formal prayer service in Virginia, to give thanks to God for His mercy and grace in bringing them safely to this new land. In his dedicatory prayer, Hunt declared, "From these very shores the Gospel shall go forth to not only this New World, but the entire world."

As part of Virginia's incorporation, the Church of England was made the colony's established church.[56] This would lend a different approach to church and religious liberty than that of the Pilgrims and Puritans of New England. Nonetheless, the more radical Puritan way would eventually influence Virginia more than Virginia would influence New England. According to Thomas Jefferson, by the time of the American Revolution, three-quarters of Virginia's population were "dissenting Protestants."[57]

The Radical Reformers

The name "Radical Reformers" was coined by George H. Williams, late Professor of Ecclesiastical History at Yale University. It became a designation for those groups, such as the Separatist Puritans, Baptists and Quakers who rejected the reforms of Luther, Zwingli and Calvin as being inadequate primarily because they all continued the idea of a state-sanctioned church that uses the strong arm of the civil government to enforce its polity and doctrine. It can also be applied to Puritans and Presbyterians who resisted the religious tyranny of monarchs and state churches.

The earliest of these groups, known as the Anabaptists, arose in Switzerland around 1536 by those who insisted that the reforms of Luther and Zwingli were not going far enough. "Anabaptist" is a Latin derivative meaning "those who re-baptize" and was the name given to this movement by their Catholic and Lutheran opponents who resented them re-baptizing their converts. Throughout Europe laws were passed making it a capital crime to be involved in re-baptizing anyone who had already been baptized as an infant by the official, state church.

These Anabaptists, or "Radical Reformers," as Williams called them, separated themselves from the state churches and formed their own "illegal" congregations made up of voluntary members. They, therefore, came under intense persecution by the state churches, both Catholic and Protestant. They were hounded, imprisoned, burned at the staked, and some even had their tongues cut out.

These Radical Reformers emphasized freedom of conscience and religious liberty. No one should be forced to act against their sincerely held religious convictions, they insisted, and there should be no governmental force in matters of faith and worship. They pointed out that this unbiblical use of force in matters of faith had begun with Constantine and his marriage of the church with the state. They insisted that this ungodly marriage had created a corrupt and false church that relied on the power of the state rather than the power of the Gospel message for its existence and expansion.

This Radical Reformation spread throughout Europe and influenced other groups that arose such as the Separatist Puritans, English Baptists and Quakers. In his writings on the Radical Reformation, Williams emphasizes the influence these groups had on the thinking of Western civilization, particularly in the areas of individual freedom and religious liberty. He wrote,

> The whole Western world, not only the direct descendants of the Continental Anabaptists, not alone even the larger Protestant community, but all who cherish Western institutions and freedoms, must acknowledge their indebtedness to the valor and the vision of the Anabaptists who glimpsed afresh the disparities between the church and the world, even when the latter construed itself as Christian.[58]

These Radical Reformers were continually in conflict with authority, both civil and religious. Out of necessity, they and their offshoots developed ideas of individual liberty and religious freedom, which they brought to the New World and further developed on American soil.

Baptists Settle Rhode Island

Roger Williams founded the first Baptist church in America, which was the First Baptist Church of Providence, Rhode Island, and still is in existence today. Born in London, probably in 1603, Williams had a spiritual conversion at a very early age, and while a student at Cambridge University he came under the influence of the Puritans.

Williams was ordained with the Church of England, but as a Puritan he came under the persecution instigated by Charles I and Archbishop Laud against all Puritans. This led to his reexamination of the church and church-state relations and he concluded that the Church of England was a harlot church and he could not be a part of it.

By the time he arrived at the Massachusetts Bay Colony in 1631, Williams had already moved to the Separatist position. Somewhere along the way he also moved to the Anabaptist position of baptizing believers at the time of their conversion experience.

Upon arrival in Boston on February 5, 1631, the Boston church invited him to become its minister, while the regular pastor, John Wilson, returned to England to fetch his wife. Realizing that the Puritans had not formally and openly renounced the Church of England, Williams caused a stir when he declined the position on grounds that it was "an unseparated church." Williams then began taking the Puritan leaders and ministers to task for what he considered a lack of commitment to Biblical truth.

Both Bradford and Winslow recognized Williams' brilliance, and both maintained friendly relations with him, even after his expulsion. Bradford hosted him for a time in Plymouth and invited him to preach to the Plymouth congregation. He later described Williams as "a man godly and zealous but very unsettled in judgment."[59]

Bradford does not go into detail concerning where Williams was "unsettled in judgment." It could be that Williams was also preaching adult believers baptism by this time. Even the Separatist Pilgrims had continued the practice of infant baptism, which had been a part of their experience as Anglicans. Rogers would have considered this to be unbiblical and a carryover from a corrupt religious system.

Returning from Plymouth to the Massachusetts Bay Colony, Williams continued to hammer the Puritan leaders for what he considered to be their compromise with the world and lack of commitment to Biblical truth. The picture of Williams as an enlightened forerunner of a free, secular society is absolutely false. Williams did not object to Massachusetts being a Christian commonwealth. His problem with Massachusetts was that, in his thinking, it was not Christian enough.

Winslow and the colony's leadership had several meetings with Williams and finally decided it would be best for him to leave the colony. In their minds, he was a religious extremist whose continued presence would be unhealthy for the colony. They gave him six weeks to depart.

Williams eventually left with five followers and founded the colony of Rhode Island, which he purchased from the native population. He also founded a city that he named "Providence," expressing his conviction that God was ordering all the circumstances of his life to bring about His will. Rhode Island became a haven for religious dissenters, particularly Baptists and Quakers, functioning with absolute freedom of conscience and religious liberty for all.

Williams' ideal of religious liberty and the freedom of the church from the state contributed to the development of ideas that would lead to America's founding documents. Like the Separatist Puritans, the separation of church and state was, for Williams, unidirectional. It simply meant no establishment of a national, state-sanctioned church that would use the power of civil government to enforce its doctrine and liturgy. It is best expressed as "the freedom of church from the state."

The situation with Williams revealed a flaw in the Puritan experiment with democracy wherein the civil government has a vested interest in the success of one particular church or denomination. In this case, it was the Congregational Church of the Puritans.

These encounters, however, had the effect of moving the Puritans toward a greater openness toward those of different theological persuasions, as is demonstrated by the fact that by the end of the century there were at least ten Baptist churches in existence in New England. By the time of the War for Independence, the Puritans had moved even closer to the Baptists in regards to church-state relations.

The Impact of the Quakers

Numerous other groups also came to America seeking freedom to express their renewed and reformed faith. The Dutch Reformed settled New York and New Jersey. Presbyterians from Scotland and Ireland settled in the same area and in Maryland. Baptists not only settled in Rhode Island, but also settled in various locations throughout the colonies. Reform minded Catholics, committed to religious tolerance, settled in Maryland.

The Quakers settled Pennsylvania and it became a haven for religious dissenters. Quakers, along with the Baptists and Separatist Puritans, were early champions of freedom of conscience and of the idea that there should be no state-sanctioned church.

The Quakers called themselves the "Religious Society of Friends," and they trace their beginning to George Fox (1624-1691), who was raised in a Puritan home in Leicestershire, England. Having a spiritual passion from his youth, he was unable to find peace and satisfaction in his soul until one day he heard a voice say, "There is one, even Christ Jesus, that can speak to thy condition."[60] Fox then began to emphasize what he called the "inner light" in place of all outward forms, rituals and regulations. The movement exploded in growth.

One of those drawn to the Quakers was William Penn, who was born in 1644 into a wealthy, aristocratic family in London, and whose parents were members of the official Anglican Church. His father was an Admiral in the British Navy and had played a prominent role in restoring the monarchy to Charles II after the death of Oliver Cromwell. His parents hoped he would follow in his father's footsteps and distinguish himself in some elite political or naval position. Their hopes, however, were dashed when young William identified himself with the lowly and despised Quakers.

The Penns owned an estate in Cork, Ireland, and while spending time there at the age of twelve, William heard the itinerant Quaker preacher, Thomas Loe, speak of a faith "that overcomes the world and a faith that is overcome by the world." Penn immediately knew that, more than anything, he wanted that faith that overcomes the world.

Penn was initially beaten by his father and rejected by both parents because of his association with the Quakers. Persecution was intense since Quakerism was considered a threat to the official church and to society, and Penn was imprisoned for a time in the Tower of London. Making good use of his time in the tower, he wrote one of his most popular works, *No Cross, No Crown*, in which he made the point that the way of the Cross, "is the only door to true Christianity."

The Quakers took church reform a step beyond the Separatist Puritans and rejected all forms of government and outward ordinances for their churches. In place of outward forms and regulations, they emphasized the inward work of the Holy Spirit in each believer and the New Testament admonition to "brotherly love." They had no clerical class of ordained ministry and considered every person equal in the sight of God. They were among the most vehement opponents of slavery.

In 1681, after the death of his parents, Penn was given Pennsylvania by Charles II as repayment of a debt owed to his father. He immediately set out to make it into a colony that would be a haven for Quakers and other persecuted groups. Penn drew up plans for the colony and hinted at how he envisioned it functioning when he planned and named its major city "Philadelphia." *Philadelphia* is derived from two words from the Greek New Testament: *phileo* meaning "love," and *adelphos*, meaning "brother"; that is, *City of Brotherly Love*.

Pennsylvania provided complete individual freedom, but individuals were expected to be Christians who would order their lives from an inward sense of Christian love and morality. It was in this context that Penn declared, "He who will not be governed by God must be ruled by tyrants."

Penn applied the Quaker principle of government—or non-government—to Pennsylvania. Minimal regulation, minimal taxation, and complete religious liberty for all, characterized Pennsylvania. When the British official, John Blackwell, came to Philadelphia in 1688 he had difficulty in locating the offices of the government. When he did locate them, they were empty, for the government council only met briefly once or twice per year, as the need arose.

To the surprise of many, the colony and the city of Philadelphia flourished. From 1680-1710, the population of Pennsylvania increased by some 24-fold, while the population of New York merely doubled during the same time period. Philadelphia became the largest city in America and held that position until 1830.

The Quakers finally relinquished control of the colony after several bloody Indian raids on distant settlements in the colony. Being pacifists, the Quakers were unwilling to take action to defend the settlers. Under pressure from their own number and well-known citizens of Philadelphia, such as Benjamin Franklin, they finally gave up control of the colony in 1756.

Nonetheless, the radical Pennsylvania experiment of religious and individual freedom had shown what can happen when a self-governed people are given the freedom to pursue their dreams under God. The Founders recognized the value of the Pennsylvania experiment. In fact, Penn's "Frame of Government" and "Charter of Privileges," which provided the constitutional guidelines for Pennsylvania's government, were studied by Benjamin Franklin and other Founding Fathers. In his excellent book, *Faith & Freedom*, Hart says,

> It would have been very difficult to explain exactly what it was Americans were fighting for if the Quakers had not in fact implemented William Penn's political philosophy: especially, that government has no right to use force against

individuals to serve the purposes of the community. There would have been no experience of such a society to point to without Pennsylvania. Quaker rule provided the needed historical precedent. They were averse to using force to an extreme. But it was the radical nature of the Quaker conception of government that led to the new political theory that would emerge between 1776 and 1787.[61]

The Quaker experiment reminds us that the freedoms enshrined in the American Constitution and Bill of Rights will only work when they are applied to a people who are self-governed by Christian principles of morality. Otherwise, freedom becomes anarchy and a means for the pursuit of selfish and ungodly ends. This is what John Adams was referring to when he said, "Our Constitution was made only for a moral and religious people. It is wholly inadequate for the government of any other."[62]

America's Christian Origins Are Undeniable

As can be seen, America was not settled by mild-mannered Christians who were tepid in their faith and reserved in their witness of that faith. These early immigrants were totally committed to Christ and were willing to make any sacrifice to advance the freedom that they believed was the God-given right of every human being. Hart expressed it well when he wrote,

It was Protestants of the most radical stripe, most zealous in their religious convictions (those whom

66

the America Civil Liberties Union would like to see outlawed from the public discourse) who were in fact the greatest proponents of religious liberty as codified in America's governing charter 200 years later.[63]

In spite of religious squabbles that, at times, erupted among the different groups, and the non-Christian behavior of some, there is no question that America's origins were rooted in a passion to recover and live out the Christianity of the New Testament. Speaking in 1820 at the 200-year anniversary celebration of the landing of the Pilgrims at Plymouth, the noted U.S. senator, Daniel Webster, said;

> Finally, let us not forget the religious character of our origin. Our fathers were brought hither by their high veneration for the Christian religion. They journeyed by its light, and labored in its hope. They sought to incorporate its principles with the elements of their society, and to diffuse its influence through all their institutions, civil, political, or literary. Let us cherish these sentiments, and extend this influence still more widely; in the full conviction, that that is the happiest society which partakes in the highest degree of the mild peaceful spirit of Christianity.[64]

God Has No Grandchildren

A wise man once said, "God has no grandchildren." In other words, there is no automatic or formal passing of genuine faith from one generation to the next. Each generation must know and experience God for themselves. This truth is clearly seen in the early American experience as the first generation passed from the scene and the children and grandchildren of those first "Pilgrims" began to establish themselves in the society which their parents had carved for them in the New World.

The Vision Wanes

> The golden showers have been restrained;
> the influences of the Spirit suspended;
> he consequence has been that the gospel
> has not had any eminent success.
> Conversions have been rare and dubious;
> few sons and daughters have been born to God.
>
> *William Cooper, Puritan Pastor*

In spite of the hardships encountered in carving out a new life in the New World, first generation immigrants to America were normally warm and vibrant in their faith and passionate in their vision for a revival of New Testament Christianity and a new nation "under God."

Their children and grandchildren, however, while retaining many of the outward forms of worship and doctrine, tended to lose the vitality and vision of their parents and grandparents. As former generations passed from the scene, the original passion for Christian reform and renewal passed with them, and succeeding generations were left with a form of godliness but lacking the power thereof (II Timothy 3:5).

This was nowhere more obvious than in New England where, by the 1650s, the original Puritan vision for the complete reformation of Christendom had obviously waned, being replaced by more worldly concerns. Even before his death in 1657, Bradford had lamented that the younger generation at Plymouth had lost the Spiritual passion and vision of their mothers and fathers.[65] Commenting on Bradford's lament, Dr. Samuel Morris, editor of Bradford's work, wrote,

> In his later years the Governor felt that the glory had departed from Plymouth; the town declining in numbers, population dispersed, young people indifferent to religion and heedless of their fathers' sacrifices, luxury coming in with prosperity.[66]

Worldly Concerns
Replace Spiritual Priorities

Whereas the faith and disciplined work ethic of the first generation Puritans had produced prosperity, for many second and third generation Puritans the prosperity itself became the goal. As the well-known Puritan pastor, Cotton Mather, put it, "Religion begat prosperity and the daughter devoured the mother."[67]

The preoccupation with acquiring earthly goods and affluence was also a factor in deteriorating relationships with the native population. Whereas the first generation of Puritans was committed to reaching the native population with the Gospel and sought to build genuine friendship, the lust for land by succeeding generations at times trumped their evangelistic zeal and led to a number of disingenuous treaties with different Indian tribes. Already suspicious of the new immigrants and their new religion, this further alienated many of the tribes and resulted in a number of bloody conflicts, which resulted in a further drain of spiritual life and vitality.

Half-Way Christians

The loss of spiritual life and vitality among the Puritans was also reflected in the "half-way covenant," which was implemented by second and third generation Puritans in 1662 in hope of impeding the alarming loss of church members. This "half-way covenant" offered partial membership to those who could not testify of a saving relationship with Jesus Christ, and it allowed these "nominal" Christians to have their children baptized without claiming full church membership. Many of the churches had thus deteriorated into formal religious institutions with no power to bring needed change.

Seventeen years later, in 1679, a group of ministers met in Massachusetts and at the conclusion of their gathering issued a statement declaring that, "God hath a controversy with His New England people." Those attending this "Reforming Synod" formulated this statement because of the increase in ungodliness and spiritual indifference they observed on every hand.

The Loss of Brotherly Love

Weaknesses in the Puritan experiment also began to appear as outsiders, such as Quakers and Baptists, who held different theological views, came into their midst. Feeling that their way of life was being threatened and undermined by these outsiders, the Puritans responded at times with harshness.

On the one hand, their response is understandable for they and their parents had sacrificed much and worked very hard to carve out a life in the New England wilderness. Should they now allow outsiders to undermine what they had established with doctrines and practices with which they did not agree? But, on the other hand, should not a Christian society allow freedom of conscience in matters of faith and worship?

That in the midst of this struggle the Puritans attempted to compromise on some level is demonstrated by the existence of several Baptist churches in New England by the beginning of the 18th century. Nonetheless, their response was too often less than Christian and those Quakers and Baptists who insisted on spreading their teachings in their midst were sometimes banned from their communities, imprisoned and in some rare situations were even hanged.

Their harsh response reflected not only the loss of spiritual life, but the inherent weakness of a society in which the civil government and a particular church are too closely aligned and use their cooperative power to coerce others in matters of faith. In New England it was the Congregational Church, the church of the Puritans, which was too closely aligned with their civil government.

In the end, the Puritan treatment of outsiders would confirm the Quaker/Baptist ideals of civil government not taking sides with any church, but being diligent to protect the free expression of faith by all sects and denominations. This would all play into the formulation, just over one hundred years later, of the First Amendment to the Constitution in which the founders would state, "Congress shall make no law concerning the establishment of religion, nor hindering the free exercise thereof."

The Witchcraft Trials

When people live as formal Christians, believing in the doctrines of the Bible but lacking the power of a personal relationship with God, they are unable to deal with attacks from the unseen world of Satan and demons. This was the case with the Puritans in the 1690s when rumors began to spread of the practice of witchcraft in their midst. When unexplained accidents then began to occur and cases of "demon possession" began to appear, they did not have the spiritual wisdom and power to deal with the situation.

Although there were isolated cases of deliverance through prayer and fasting,[68] for the most part, the people reacted in fear and relied on the civil authorities to deal with the situation. And so began the darkest period of Puritan history, the Salem witchcraft trials of 1692-93 in which over 150 people were arrested and twenty eventually found guilty and nineteen hanged for practicing witchcraft.

These proceedings have been seized upon by Puritan haters and used to paint the Puritans with a broad brush in hopes of destroying their reputation and undermining their positive influence in the founding of this nation. It should be remembered, however, that this was an isolated incident that took place in one small community. Mark Noll has pointed out that, compared with what was happening in Europe at the time, the actions of the Puritans were quite guarded, for hundreds of supposed witches were executed in Europe during this same period at the behest of both Catholics and Protestants.[69]

It was eventually the protest of Puritan pastors such as Increase Mather that brought an end to the proceedings. Later, one of the judges at the trials, Samuel Sewall, made a public statement lamenting his actions lest some innocent person had been condemned. He asked for God's forgiveness for himself and for all New England.[70] Nonetheless, a dark cloud of uncertainty and disillusionment was cast over all New England.

Prayers for a Divine Awakening

By the end of the century, Winthrop's vision of New England being a "shining light" and a "city on a hill" for the churches of Europe seemed very dim indeed. Not only were many of the existing churches spiritually dead, but many areas, because of rapid population growth, were without churches or pastors. Sabbath breaking, profanity, gambling, and lewdness seemed to be everywhere.

As a new century dawned, many ministers and laypeople alike were deeply concerned about the immorality and spiritual indifference that seemed to pervade the land and the churches. One pastor described it as a "dead and barren time" and went on to say,

> The golden showers have been restrained; the influences of the Spirit suspended; the consequence has been that the gospel has not had any eminent success. Conversions have been rare and dubious; few sons and daughters have been born to God; and the hearts of Christians not so quickened, warmed, and refreshed under the ordinances, as they have been.[71]

The spiritual condition of the populace was so bleak that calls for special times of prayer and fasting began to be issued throughout the colonies by both pastors and government officials. William Cooper, a pastor from New England, recalled that before the Great Awakening there was "a constant petition in our public prayers, from Sabbath to Sabbath, that God would pour out His Spirit upon us and revive his work in the midst of the years."[72]

He also stated that most of the churches had "set apart days, wherein to seek the Lord by prayer and fasting." In addition to these times of fasting and prayer set by the churches, there were "annual fast days appointed by the government."[73]

Would God be faithful to answer the prayers of His people? Would He honor the faith and sacrifice of their forefathers and foremothers? Would He demonstrate that He had a plan for this land?

The Great Awakening

The work of God, as it was carried on,
and the number of true saints multiplied,
soon made a glorious alteration in the town:
so that in the spring and summer following,
anno 1735, the town seemed to be
full of the presence of God.

Jonathan Edwards

By 1726, it was obvious that the prayers of the people
were beginning to be answered when revival erupted
among the Dutch Reformed of New Jersey. It began as
the result of a young Dutch Reformed pastor, Theodore
Frelinghuysen, visiting his flock in their homes and
boldly pointing out, both in person and from the pulpit,
their un-Christian behavior and their spiritual apathy.
He preached about the reality of sin and the grace of the
Gospel, and he called upon his people to take their faith
seriously.

In the beginning, some were offended, and separated
from him, but eventually his preaching bore fruit as a
powerful revival began to spread among the churches he
pastored. In later years when George Whitefield visited

that area, he acknowledged the work of Frelinghuysen and said of him, "He is a worthy soldier of Jesus Christ, and was the beginner of the great work which I trust the Lord is carrying on in these parts."[74]

Gilbert Tennent

One of those impacted by Frelinghuysen was Gilbert Tennent (1703-1764), a young Presbyterian pastor in the town of New Brunswick, New Jersey. Gilbert had been born in County Armagh, Ireland, in 1703. At the age of fourteen, he immigrated with his parents and three brothers to America, settling in Bucks County, Pennsylvania, where his father, William, took the pastorate of the Neshaminy Presbyterian Church. It was here that Gilbert and his brothers received the training that would prepare them as some of the most prominent preachers of the Great Awakening.

Gilbert's father, William, had been trained at the University of Edinburgh and was a Biblical scholar, well versed in Hebrew, Greek and Latin. He was also a man of piety who emphasized the importance of a vital faith that is both known in the head and experienced in the heart.

One of his first acts after getting settled in his new home, was to erect a log building approximately twenty feet long and twenty feet wide where he began classes with thirteen students, including Gilbert and his three brothers. Years later when George Whitefield visited the area and preached to approximately three-thousand in the "meeting-house yard," he described the Log College as being like the "old school of the prophets." Many historians consider the Log College to be the forerunner of Princeton University.[75]

After graduating from the Log College, Gilbert was licensed to preach by the Presbyterian Church and settled into a pastorate in New Brunswick, New Jersey. Shortly after assuming this pastorate, Gilbert became deathly ill and wondered if his life might be over. Feeling that he had accomplished so little in his service to God, Gilbert promised God that if He would allow him just six more months, he would, "Stand upon the stage of the world, as it were, and plead more faithfully for his cause, and take more earnest pains for the salvation of souls."[76]

Gilbert experienced a transformation of his health and began to preach with a new urgency. He began to boldly point out the hypocrisy and the shallowness of faith among those in his congregation and insisted on a true conversion experience that is rooted solely in faith in Jesus Christ.

Gilbert's new sense of urgency and the boldness with which he confronted sin and hypocrisy led some to refer to him as a "Son of Thunder." Although he encountered some opposition, a deep concern for their spiritual state gripped his congregation and the revival began to impact his community.

It was during this time that Gilbert met Theodore Frelinghuysen and saw the revival that was taking place in his Dutch Reformed congregations. They were able to encourage each other, and revival began to spread throughout the middle colonies. When George Whitefield visited the area in 1739, he said of Gilbert, "He and his associates are now the burning and shining lights of this part of America."[77]

With the Awakening spreading to various communities, Gilbert began to travel to other communities boldly proclaiming the importance of a "new birth" through faith in Jesus Christ. Everywhere he went multitudes were awakened to the fact that they could not trust in the religion of their parents, church membership, or their own good works, but must put their faith completely in Christ.

Gilbert also challenged the clergy with a scathing message entitled "The Danger of an Unconverted Ministry" in which he compared many colonial church leaders with the Pharisees of Jesus' day, pious and proud in their own righteousness but opposing the genuine work of God in their midst.

On one of his preaching tours through Philadelphia, George Whitefield met the Tennents and recognized their significant contribution to the Awakening. He asked Gilbert to take a preaching tour and "water the seed" in all the places where he had preached the Word. Gilbert agreed and everywhere he travelled he saw an amazing response to his message. One writer has said, "Preaching almost every day for three months, Tennent witnessed a "shaking among the dry bones." [78]

Gilbert followed Whitefield to Boston about three months after Whitefield had departed in September of 1740. He spent about three months there and the results were astounding. One eyewitness wrote,

The December following Mr. G. Tennent arrived whose preaching was followed by still greater effects ... . On Monday March 2, 1741, Mr. Tennent preached his farewell sermon to an extremely crowded and deeply affected audience. "And now was a time such as we never knew. Mr. Cooper was wont to say, that more came to him in one week in deep concern about their souls, than in the whole twenty-four years of his previous ministry."[79]

Jonathan Edwards
And Revival in New England

As revival was spreading throughout the middle colonies, it also began to break forth in New England among the descendants of the Puritans. Jonathan Edwards (1703-1758), pastor of the Congregational Church in Northampton, Massachusetts, had been concerned by what he described as "the general deadness throughout the land," and he and his wife, Sarah, had set themselves to seek God for a "revival of religion."[80]

Edwards was a child prodigy who entered Yale College at the age of thirteen and graduated four years later as class valedictorian at the age of seventeen. He was a diligent student of Scripture, and became versed in the ancient languages. In addition to being a studious person, he was also a person with a tender heart towards the Lord who could be melted to tears while contemplating the love and mercy of God. When George Whitefield preached in the Northampton church he noted in his *Journal*, "The good Mr. Edwards wept throughout the sermon."[81]

As Jonathan, Sarah and others prayed, an unusual sense of God's presence seemed to fill the entire community of Northampton during the spring and summer of 1735. Edwards reported, "The town seemed to be full of the presence of God." In every part of town, the Spirit of God was powerfully at work until "there was scarcely a single person in the town, old or young, left unconcerned about the great things of the eternal world."[82]

Without any sort of planned evangelistic outreach, "souls did as it were come by flocks to Jesus Christ."[83] Instead of resorting to the tavern, people now crowded Edwards' home clamoring to hear the message of Christ and His salvation. His home, Edwards said, "was thronged far more than ever the tavern had been wont to be."[84]

The Spirit of God worked so powerfully that "the tavern was soon left empty."[85] "A loose, careless person could scarcely be found," said Edwards, "And if there was anyone that seemed to remain senseless or unconcerned it would be spoken of as a *strange* thing."[86]

Without any special church growth emphases or human attempts to increase the attendance, the church in Northampton suddenly filled with those seeking salvation and with those experiencing the fruit of already having been born again. Edwards wrote,

> Our public assemblies were then beautiful: the congregation was alive in God's service, everyone intent on the public worship, every hearer eager to drink in the words of the minister as they came from his mouth; the assembly were in general from time to time in tears while the word was preached;

some weeping with sorrow and distress, others with joy and love, others with pity and concern for the souls of their neighbors.[87]

People from other communities often scoffed when they heard of the events in Northampton. But when they visited Northampton, their skepticism vanished in the overwhelming sense of God's presence. Edwards wrote,

Strangers were generally surprised to find things so much beyond what they had heard, and were wont to tell others that the state of the town could not be conceived by those who had not seen it.[88]

As converts returned home, they carried the spirit of revival with them, and the Awakening spread. The Awakening also spontaneously sprang up in other communities, apart from any contact with Northampton. In Hatfield, the whole town was at once "seized" with a concern about the things of God and salvation through Jesus Christ. It also appeared in Sunderland and soon "overspread the town." A Rev. Bull of Westfield informed Edwards that there had been a transformation of his town and that "more had been done in one week than in seven years before."[89]

It was during this time that Edwards preached his famous sermon, "Sinners in the Hands of an Angry God" at a church in Enfield, Connecticut. As he preached, the justice of God and the reality of eternal punishment became so real to the congregation that some clutched the backs of pews while others wrapped their arms around the pillars to keep, as it were, from falling into hell and being consumed by its eternal flames. Edwards' voice was drowned out by the prayers and cries for mercy that spontaneously sprang forth from the congregation. "He made hell real enough to be found in the atlas," said Edwards' biographer, Ola Winslow.[90]

The response could not be attributed to Edwards' preaching style, for he was neither loud nor flamboyant in his presentation. A very logical and studious personality, he wrote out all his sermons in a manuscript. He then stood behind the podium, and without moving or making any physical gestures, he would read his sermon in a monotone voice. Being nearsighted, he held the manuscript so close to his face that the congregation could not see his face. His example is a reminder that we must not associate the power of the Holy Spirit with the noise, glitz, and glitter of Christian entertainment.

The Message Made the Difference

What made the difference was not the act or style of preaching, but it was, instead, the message that was preached. This understanding is critical, for in Romans 1:16, Paul speaks of the inherent power of the Gospel Message and warns that, if we go too far in attempting to make the Message "cool, hip and acceptable" to contemporary culture, we run the risk of preaching a Gospel that has been *emptied of its power* (I Corinthians 1:17 NIV).

Recovering the purity of the Gospel Message was, in fact, a primary goal of the Protestant Reformation, beginning with Martin Luther. This was also a goal of Edwards and the preachers of the Great Awakening. They had rejected tradition, and they desired, more than anything, to preach the Message of Jesus and the New Testament. The Message they preached may be summarized as follows:

1. God is a great, majestic and holy Being who created all things and to whom all creatures owe their love, honor, and respect.

2. The man and woman whom God created in His image and likeness, rebelled against their Creator, dragging their posterity down with them into the abyss of sin and judgment, into what, in historical theology, is known as "the fall."

3. The human race in its current state is a rebellious and fallen race, separated from God, under the power of sin and deserving of hell.

4. God in His sovereign mercy and grace now offers full pardon and forgiveness of sin to all who will put their faith in Jesus Christ, the Savior, whom God sent to die on the cross for our sins and to rise again for our salvation.

5. Get rid of faulty foundations. They emphasized that many professing Christians had built their faith on faulty foundations, such as church membership, good deeds, family pedigree, social status, and cultural refinement. They emphasized that these old foundations must be overturned and faith in Jesus Christ alone must be laid as the only foundation for acceptance with God.

6. There must be a new birth. They emphasized that

when one truly believes in Christ there is a work of regeneration by the Holy Spirit that occurs in the heart—a new birth—from which springs new desires and aspirations that are godly, producing a whole new tenor of life.

7. They emphasized the eternal bliss in heaven for all who trust in Christ and the eternal suffering and separation from God of all who refuse God's gracious gift of salvation in Christ.

The Message preached, backed by much prayer, was the key to the amazing impact of the Great Awakening. The preachers of the Awakening grappled in prayer and study to identify and articulate the Message they preached—a Message that brought them much persecution and rejection from the religious *status quo*.

Nonetheless, their Message prevailed, and Colonial America was transformed. The well-known English pastor, theologian, and hymn writer, Isaac Watts, read Edwards' account of how the Awakening had transformed New England and was greatly inspired. He wrote,

We are taught by this happy event how easy it will be for our blessed Lord to make a full accomplishment of all His predictions concerning His kingdom, and to spread His dominion from sea to sea, through all the nations of the earth. We see how easy it is for Him with one turn of His hand, with one word of His mouth, to awaken whole countries of stupid and sleeping sinners, and kindle divine life in their souls.[91]

The Marginalized Of Society Are Awakened

The power of God seemed to descend upon
the assembly 'like a mighty raging wind,'
and with an astonishing energy bore down
all before it. They were almost universally
praying and crying for mercy in every part
of the house, and many out of doors;
and numbers could neither go nor stand.
I thought this had a near resemblance
to the day of God's power,
mentioned in Josh. 10: 14;
for I must say I never saw any day like it.

*David Brainerd, describing the Awakening
among the Delaware Indians of New Jersey*

The preachers of the Great Awakening saw everyone, regardless of race, class or gender, under the power and penalty of sin with only one remedy, that being, faith in Jesus Christ. Social standing, the possession or absence of wealth, whether male or female, and whether slave or free—all of these factors were all irrelevant when it came to forgiveness of sins through faith in Jesus Christ.

Moved by this theological understanding and stirred by the power of the Awakening, many began to reach across cultural divides to share the Good News with those who had been relegated to the margins of colonial American society. As a result, women, African-Americans, and Native Americans all shared in the benefits and power of the Awakening.

The Awakening Impacts Women

One writer has pointed out that, although critics of the Awakening took umbrage with the emotional excesses they believed they observed, they were even more incensed when "some white women and African Americans shed their subordinate social status long enough to exhort religious gatherings."[92]

Sarah Pierpont Edwards would be a case in point. When the Awakening came to Northampton, she was so powerfully affected that, at times, she was unable to stand, and, at other times, she experienced great joy in the conscious presence of the Holy Spirit. She writes, "I could scarcely refrain from leaping with transports of joy."[93]

This sort of dynamic experience of the Spirit's presence moved her to act outside the traditional roles of wife and mother and to exhort others concerning the things of God. She not only discussed Biblical and theological themes with her husband and visiting ministers, but at times, she exhorted others out of the overflow of her own experience. For example, she told of hearing a visiting minister lament that God's children should be cold and lifeless in their faith, and then shared her amazing response. She said,

> I felt such a sense of the deep ingratitude manifested by the children of God, in such coldness and deadness, that my strength was immediately taken away, and I sunk down on the spot. Those who were near raised me, and placed me in a chair; and, from the fullness of my heart, I expressed to them, in a very earnest manner, the deep sense I had of the wonderful grace of Christ towards me, of the assurance I had of his having saved me from hell, of my happiness running parallel with eternity, of the duty of giving up all to God, and of the peace and joy inspired by an entire dependence on his mercy and grace.[94]

Moved, perhaps in part, by his wife's experiences, Jonathan Edwards, considered by many to be the greatest theologian/philosopher America has produced, developed views on gender that were obviously ahead of his time. His commentary on Eve being the "the mother of all living" has been construed by some scholars as an indication that he held "proto-feminist" views, and one writer has described him as being "genuinely committed to the promotion of gender equality." The Edwards apparently reared their daughters with a sense of equality, for one biographer, in describing the character of their daughter, Esther, said, "She was used to being taken seriously as the spiritual and intellectual equal of men."[95]

These currents of equality are always present in

movements of spiritual renewal where more value is placed on the Spirit's presence and power for teaching and ministry than on more traditional criteria, such as one's gender. This sort of gender equality that is rooted in the Spirit was at full bloom among the Quakers and to a lesser extent among the Baptists of colonial America. The Puritan culture had given women more freedom than most cultures and religions of the day, but still confined them primarily to roles of motherhood and homemaker.[96]

Nonetheless, the way was opened for women to play some very prominent roles in the American Revolution.[97] In addition, ripples of equality were set loose that would grow into a spiritual tsunami in the Second Great Awakening of the next century, out of which would emerge the suffrage movement and the great fight for both gender and racial equality.[98]

The Awakening Impacts Native Americans

Relationships with the native population had been strained because of the lust for land on the part of second and third generation Puritans and because many native chiefs and medicine men saw the new settlers and their new religion as threats to their own power and influence. These tensions had led to some very brutal conflicts in the latter part of the 1600s, and these served to further widen the chasm between the two peoples.

Nonetheless, moved by the power of the Awakening and its central theme that all people are separated from God by sin and in need of salvation through Christ, a number of ardent souls began to reach out to the Indians in kindness and at great personal sacrifice. As a result, a powerful work of the Holy Spirit was begun among the native population.

A case in point is David Brainerd (1718-1747) who worked with the Mohicans, Stockbridge and Susquehanna of Massachusetts, and the Delaware of New Jersey and Pennsylvania. Although his brief missionary career was cut short by the onset of tuberculosis and his untimely death at the age of twenty-nine, Brainerd's missionary passion and dedication became an example for many after his *Journal* was published by Jonathan Edwards shortly after his death in the Edwards' home.

Giving himself completely to his task, Brainerd studied the native language so that he could share portions of the Gospel and the Psalms in their own language. In the wilderness where he was often alone and without necessary sustenance, he gave himself to fervent prayer for the natives and often set aside entire days for prayer and fasting. His *Journal* entry for April 19, 1742, reads,

> I set apart this day for fasting and prayer to God for his grace; especially to prepare me for the work of the ministry; to give me divine aid and direction in my preparations for that great work; and in his own time to send me into his harvest. In the forenoon I felt the power of intercession for precious, immortal souls; for the advancement of the kingdom of my dear Lord and Savior in the world . . . God enabled me so to agonize in prayer

that I was quite wet with sweat, though in the shade and the cool wind. My soul was drawn out very much for the world; I grasped for multitudes of souls.[99]

It was while ministering to the Delaware at a place called Crossweeksung, New Jersey, that Brainerd began to see his prayers answered in a remarkable way. In his *Journal* dated August 8, 1745, he wrote,

The power of God seemed to descend upon the assembly 'like a mighty raging wind,' and with an astonishing energy bore down all before it. I stood amazed at the influence which seized the audience almost universally; and could compare it to nothing more aptly than the irresistible force of a mighty torrent, or swelling deluge, that with its insupportable weight and pressure bears down and sweeps before it whatever is in its way. The most stubborn hearts were now obliged to bow. A principal man among the Indians . . . was now brought under solemn concern for his soul, and wept bitterly. They were almost universally praying and crying for mercy in every part of the house, and many out of doors; and numbers could neither go nor stand. Their concern was so great, each one for himself, that none seemed to take any notice of those about them, but each prayed freely for himself. I thought this had a near resemblance to the day of God's power, mentioned in Josh. 10: 14; for I must say I never saw any day like it, in all respects: it was a day wherein I am persuaded the

Lord did much to destroy the kingdom of darkness among this people.[100]

A thriving Christian church and community emerged among the Delaware with Brainerd raising money to guarantee that their land was secured and would never be taken. He wrote of his beloved Indian congregation,

> I know of no assembly of Christians, where there seems to be so much of the presence of God, where brotherly love so much prevails, and where I should take so much delight in the public worship of God in general, as in my own congregation.[101]

Although he died two years later of tuberculosis, others carried on Brainerd's work, including his brother John. Jonathan Edwards, in whose home Brainerd passed away, was so impressed with Brainerd's life and work that he published his *Journal*, which to this day continues to inspire many to an unreserved commitment to God and His service. No doubt inspired by Brainerd's example, Edwards himself later became a missionary to the Housatonic Indians in the area of Stockbridge, Massachusetts.

Even John Wesley was so impressed by reading Brainerd's *Journal* that he had it distributed to all his Methodist societies and instructed his preachers to, "Read carefully over the life of David Brainerd."

When the Revolutionary War broke out, the British were able to persuade many Indian tribes to join their side of the conflict through promises of land guarantees, claims of military superiority and certain victory over the colonists. Nonetheless, a substantial number of Native Americans joined the colonists against the British. Interestingly, many were from the very areas where Brainerd, Edwards, and others had seen the most success, such as in Stockbridge in western Massachusetts and from throughout New England.

The Oneidas and Tuscaroras, who were tribes in the Middle Colonies and also part of the Iroquois nation, sided with the Colonists, owing in large measure to the efforts of their Presbyterian missionary, Samuel Kirkland.[102] These and other Native Americans volunteered as Minutemen, and they joined Washington's army at the siege of Boston, and served in New York, New Jersey, and other areas of conflict.

The Awakening Impacts African-Americans

Because of the understanding that all people are under the power of sin and in need of Christ, a number of evangelists of the Awakening targeted blacks, both slave and free, in their preaching. Their message of a personal "new birth" experience with God resonated with the black populace, which also found many areas of Scripture with which they could identify, such as Israel's time of slavery in Egypt and God's mighty deliverance of them. The records indicate that there was indeed a Great Awakening among the black populace at this time.

Gilbert Tennent, for example, was delighted that during a preaching tour in Massachusetts, "multitudes were awakened, and several received great consolation, especially among the young people, children, and 'Negroes.'"[103]

Jonathan Edwards, in his account of the Awakening in his hometown of Northampton, mentions "several negroes" who appeared to have been truly born again.[104]

After preaching his farewell message in Philadelphia and retiring to his lodging, George Whitefield reported that, "Near 50 Negroes came to give me thanks for what God had done for their souls." Whitefield considered this an answer to prayer, saying, "I have been much drawn in prayer for them, and have seen them wrought upon by the word preached." [105]

One black woman who had been converted under Whitefield's ministry became discouraged and prayed that the Lord would manifest Himself to her on a particular day when a Baptist minister was preaching. Whitefield said that the word came with such power that the woman began to cry out and "could not help praising and blessing God." When some criticized her for interrupting the preacher, Whitefield came to her defense saying he believed that in that hour, "the Lord Jesus took a great possession of her soul."[106] He went on to say, "I doubt not, when the poor Negroes are to be called, God will highly favor them, to wipe off their reproach, and show that He is no respecter of persons."[107]

Whitefield's impact among the black populace of colonial America is indicated by the moving tribute that a black woman, Phillis Wheatley, who later became America's first published black poet, wrote in his honor at the time of his death. Her words express the strains of equality that were heard in the Gospel he preached. It reads in part,

Thou didst in strains of eloquence refined,
Inflame the heart and captivate the mind.
The greatest gift that even God can give,
He freely offered to the numerous throng.
Take him, ye Africans, he longs for you,
Impartial Savior is his title due.

Wheatley obviously quoted directly from Whitefield's preaching in her poem. Knowing Whitefield's passionate form of preaching, one can picture him crying out to blacks in his audience, "Take him, ye Africans, he longs for you."

This must have been the case in Philadelphia where many blacks attended his outdoor meetings. One black woman, after hearing Whitefield, stated that he must have been in a trance and insisted that "Jesus Christ must have told him what to speak to the people or else he could not speak as he did."[108]

Further south, Samuel Davies, who was a colleague of Gilbert Tennent, gave special attention to blacks, including slaves, during his time of ministry in Virginia. Davies not only preached to blacks but invited them to share in regular church observances including the Lord's Supper. In 1757 he wrote,

> What little success I have lately had, has been chiefly among the extremes of Gentlemen and Negroes. Indeed, God has been remarkably working among the latter. I have baptized 150 adults; and at the last sacramental solemnity, I had the pleasure of seeing the table graced with sixty black faces.[109]

Although some have criticized some of the revivalists for not being more outright in their opposition to the institution of slavery, we must remember that they lived and preached in the light of eternity. For them, this life was a passing phenomenon, and what really mattered was being ready for the next world. In their thinking, a slave on his way to heaven was far better off than a king on his way to hell.

The Awakening produced very positive results for the African-American people. It led to the emergence of many new, black congregations, among those who were enslaved and those who were free. Blacks were "humanized," and many of them identified with the struggle for freedom from Great Britain and became part of the patriotic protests, especially in New England.

At the time of the Boston Massacre in April of 1770, a black man, Crispus Attucks, was one of the leaders in the protests against the occupation of Boston by British troops. An escaped slave who had settled in Boston, he was one of those of those killed that day by British soldiers. A poem written in his honor referred to him as,

> Leader and voice that day;
> the first to defy and the first to die.[110]

The positive ripples from the Awakening also opened the way for blacks to later serve in the Revolutionary War. David Barton has provided documentation showing that numbers of blacks were given honorable discharges and pensions, and some were honored with complete military funerals for their service in the War.[111]

The Awakening also released currents of anti-slavery sentiments because, as Hart has noted, "Among the most ardent opponents of slavery were ministers, particularly the Puritan and revivalist preachers."[112] The opposition to slavery was so strong in the North that when separation with Great Britain came in 1776, immediately, several states, including Pennsylvania, Massachusetts, Connecticut, Rhode Island, Vermont, New Hampshire and New York took steps to abolish slavery, something they could not do under King George III.

Although there was more resistance in the South, where a monetary motive prevailed, the anti-slavery sentiments released by the Awakening flowered into the abolition movement of the next century, which, as Dr. Timothy Smith has shown, had its roots in American revivalism, starting with the First Great Awakening.[113]

Chapter 8

America's Spiritual Founding Father

> The multitudes of all sects and denominations
> that attended his sermons were enormous,
> and it was a matter of speculation to me,
> who was one of the number, to observe the
> extraordinary influence of his oratory on his hearers.
> From being thoughtless or indifferent about religion,
> it seemed as if all the world were growing religious
> so that one could not walk through the town
> in an evening without hearing psalms sung
> in different families of every street.
>
> *Benjamin Franklin*

George Whitefield (1714–1770) was used by God to bring all the individual flames of revival together into one Divine blaze of Spiritual Awakening.

Whitefield was uniquely prepared for his role as the firebrand of the Awakening. He was a graduate of Oxford University and an ordained minister with the Church of England. At Oxford, Whitefield had come under the tutelage of John and Charles Wesley and had experienced a dramatic conversion that forever changed his life. As part of the Methodist revival, he was exposed to the pietistic influences of Puritanism, for in a sense, Methodism was a revival of Puritanism. Both the paternal and maternal grandparents of John and Charles Wesley had been Puritan ministers and their mother's father, Dr. Samuel Annesley, was known as "the St. Paul of the nonconformists."

Whitefield's gifted preaching ability drew huge crowds. Anglican churches overflowed as multitudes came out to hear the "boy preacher." When some rectors closed their pulpits to him because of the evangelical message he preached, Whitefield was undaunted and preached in the open air to crowds numbering, at times, in the tens of thousands. When the mayor of one city opposed his outdoor meeting because it was held on "unconsecrated ground," Whitefield replied,

> Honored sir, give me leave to inform you, that God is not now confined to places, but seeketh such to worship Him, who worship in spirit and in truth. Where two or three are gathered together in Christ's Name, there will Christ be in the midst of them. The Church, by our ministers in their prayer before their sermons, is defined to be, not the church walls, but a congregation of Christian people. Such is mine.[114]

America Transformed by Spiritual Awakening

Sensing a Divine call to America, Whitefield departed England in August of 1739 with a burden for the colonists and a prayer that they would not live as thirteen scattered colonies, but as "one nation under God."[115] As he travelled up and down the eastern seaboard, shop keepers closed their doors, farmers left their plows, and workers threw down their tools to hurry to the place where he was to preach.

Crowds of ten thousand and more were common. At a time when the population of Boston was estimated at twenty thousand, Whitefield preached to an estimated crowd of 25,000 on the Boston Common. Through his incessant travels he became the best known and most recognized figure in colonial America.

When Whitefield preached in Middletown, Connecticut, Nathan Cole gave a vivid description of the stir it caused throughout the region. He was working in his field twelve miles away in Kensington when someone came along and told him that Whitefield would be preaching in Middletown at 10 o'clock that same morning.

Cole immediately dropped his tools, ran to the house, and told wife to get ready to go and hear Whitefield preach. He then saddled their horse, they both mounted, and hurried on their way to Middletown. Concerned that the horse might tire carrying two riders that distance, Cole would ride for a while and then dismount and run alongside.

As they approached the main road from Hartford to Middletown, they saw an amazing sight. A cloud of dust rose above the hills and trees and they heard a sound like a low rumbling thunder. As they drew closer they realized that the dust and sound was caused by a massive company of horses and riders on their way to hear Whitefield preach. No one made a sound and there was something surreal about the scene as every rider seemed somber and intent on his purpose. "It made me tremble to see the sight," said Cole. He went on to say,

> When we got to the Middletown old meeting house there was a great multitude, which was said to be three or four thousand people assembled together. I turned and looked towards the great river and saw the ferry boats running swift bringing over loads of people. The land and banks over the river looked black with people and horses all along the 12 miles. I saw no man at work in his field, but all seemed to be gone. When I saw Mr. Whitefield come upon the scaffold he looked almost angelical; a young, slim, slender youth before some thousands of people with a bold undaunted countenance. And my hearing how God was with him everywhere he came along, it solemnized my mind and put me into a trembling fear before he began to preach, for he looked as if he was clothed with authority from the Great God, and a sweet, solemn solemnity sat upon his brow. And my hearing him preach gave me a heart wound. By God's blessings, my old foundation was broken up, and I saw that my righteousness would not save me.

Entire Communities Transformed

Whitefield became a close friend of Benjamin Franklin and stayed in his home during his visits to Philadelphia.

Franklin's testimony of the power of the revival is particularly significant since he did not profess to be a Christian at the time. In his *Autobiography*, he tells of the incredible change that came over his hometown of Philadelphia when Whitefield came there on his first of seven visits to America. He wrote,

> The multitudes of all sects and denominations that attended his sermons were enormous, and it was a matter of speculation to me, who was one of the number, to observe the extraordinary influence of his oratory on his hearers. From being thoughtless or indifferent about religion, it seemed as if all the world were growing religious so that one could not walk through the town in an evening without hearing psalms sung in different families of every street.[116]

Franklin admits that he was skeptical of reports of Whitefield's preaching being heard by crowds of 25,000 and more. While listening to Whitefield preach from the top of the Philadelphia courthouse steps to a huge throng, Franklin, having an enquiring and scientific mind, retired backward to see how far Whitefield's voice would reach. He then did some calculations and decided that Whitefield's voice, which he described as "loud and clear," could be heard by crowds of thirty thousand and more.[117]

The Awakening Touches All Sects and Denominations

Although ordained with the state Church of England,

Whitefield did not have a denominational bone in his body. He freely fellowshipped with all true believers, including Methodists, Presbyterians, Baptists, Quakers, and any who honored God and confessed Jesus Christ as the true Lord of the Church.

In one of his sermons, as he was preaching in the open air to several thousand, representing various sects and denominations, Whitefield pretended to converse with Father Abraham, whom he pictured as looking over the banister of heaven at the gathered multitude.

Whitefield cried out, "Father Abraham, are there any Anglicans in heaven?"

The answer came back, "No, there are no Anglicans in heaven."

"Father Abraham, are there any Methodists in heaven?"

"No, there are no Methodists in heaven."

"Are there any Presbyterians in heaven?"

"No, there are no Presbyterians here either."

"What about Baptists or Quakers?"

"No, there are none of those here either."

"Father Abraham," cried Whitefield, "What kind of people are in heaven?"

The answer came back, "There are only Christians in heaven, only those who are washed in the blood of the Lamb."

Whitefield then cried out, "Oh, is that the case? Then God help me, God help us all, to forget having names and to become Christians in deed and in truth!"[118]

Although accounts of his meetings often describe the multitudes as standing and listening in rapt silence, accounts also reveal intense emotional responses at times, as things eternal were made real to their hearts and minds. On one occasion after preaching to a huge throng gathered outdoors, Whitfield surveyed the crowd and noted the amazing response. He later wrote in his *Journal*,

> Look where I would, most were drowned in tears. Some were struck pale as death, others wringing their hands, others lying on the ground, others sinking into the arms of their friends and most lifting up their eyes to heaven and crying out to God.[119]

The Vision Renewed

When preaching in New England, Whitefield called on the populace to return to the faith of their forefathers and foremothers who had originally settled that land. This deeply touched the masses who were very aware of the faith and sacrifices of their ancestors, and there is evidence they did return to that original vision of a Christian nation.

In 1756, for example, Benjamin Franklin, who had been born into a Puritan family in Boston, wrote a letter to Whitefield proposing that they partner together in establishing a new colony in Ohio that would honor God and advance the Christian faith. He wrote,

I imagine we could do it effectually and without putting the nation at too much expense. What a glorious thing it would be, to settle in that fine country a large strong body of religious and industrious people! What a security to the other colonies; and advantage to Britain, by increasing her people, territory, strength and commerce. Might it not greatly facilitate the introduction of *pure religion* among the heathen, if we could, by such a colony, show them a better sample of Christians than they commonly see in our Indian traders, the most vicious and abandoned wretches of our nation?[120]

Comparing his life to a drama and himself in the "final act," Franklin explained that he would like to "finish handsomely" by giving himself to such a project. "In such an enterprise," he said, "I could finish my life with pleasure, and I firmly believe God would bless us with success."

Franklin's proposal sounds eerily similar to the founding documents of the earliest Puritan communities of New England, which gave honor to God and expressed a desire to spread the Christian faith. Having been reared in New England, Franklin would have been intimately acquainted with its history. His proposal indicates a return in his thinking to his Puritan roots and a return to the vision of his Puritan forebears for a Christian nation.

Although time, distance, and circumstances did not allow them to ever attempt this venture, I suggest that Franklin's vision for a Christian colony did not die but was later fulfilled in a manner beyond anything he could have imagined.[121] Twenty years after the date of the above proposal, Franklin, with fifty-five others, signed the Declaration of Independence and brought into existence a new nation built on Christian values of faith and freedom.

Whitefield Burns Out for God

Although a native of England, Whitefield became best known for his ministry in America's First Great Awakening. He loved America and made seven visits to this land. A tireless worker, he travelled incessantly from Georgia to Maine preaching primarily in the open air and raising money for his beloved orphanage, Bethesda, which he had founded in Georgia. He died during his final visit to America at the age of 58, probably of congestive heart failure brought on by fatigue.

During his seventh and final visit in 1770, Whitefield was continuing his incessant travels even though he had been experiencing weakness, pain in his chest and had been coughing up blood. On September 29 he preached near Newburyport, Massachusetts, and then retired to the home of a friend, Reverend Jonathan Parsons, to spend the night.

His sleep was restless and he awakened in the middle of the night with an asthma attack. He was well enough, however, to talk of whether to winter in Boston or hasten southward. He then went back to sleep but awakened later with a tight chest and difficulty breathing. He finally stopped breathing altogether and despite a doctor's attempts to revive him, he expired at 6 A.M. on September 30, 1770.

Offers to bury him came from New Hampshire and from Boston's Old South Church. Parsons, however, quickly arranged for Whitefield's interment in the vault of the Newburyport Presbyterian Church, where his remains still lie today.

Daniel Rogers, who had been converted under Whitefield's ministry thirty years before and had remained a loyal friend, prayed at the funeral. He said that he owed his conversion "to the labors of that dear man of God, whose precious remains now lay before them." Rogers then began weeping and crying, "O my father, my father!" The congregation melted into tears.[122]

Condolences poured in from throughout the colonies and from Great Britain. Franklin was in London at the time of Whitefield's death. When he received word of his friend's passing, he wrote,

> I knew him intimately upwards of thirty years; his integrity, disinterestedness, and indefatigable zeal in prosecuting every good work, I have never seen equaled, I shall never see exceeded.[123]

Benjamin Franklin, the skeptical printer of Philadelphia, and America, would never be the same as a result of the "indefatigable zeal" of George Whitefield in preaching the Gospel to colonial America. This is why Thomas S. Kidd, Professor of History at Baylor University, has referred to Whitefield as "America's Spiritual Founding Father."[124]

Whitefield's Contribution to Independence

Whitefield, by his incessant travels, helped make the Great Awakening America's first national event. It was the first time the scattered colonists of various denominational and theological persuasions had participated together in a single event. Denominational walls were broken down, and for the first time, the colonists began to see themselves as a single people with one Divine destiny, "One Nation Under God," as Whitfield had prayed.

The preaching of Whitefield and other revivalists of the Great Awakening also helped democratize the inhabitants of the colonies by showing no preference based on wealth, class or social status. Everyone was on the same level, that is, guilty sinners before God, with only one solution for the sin problem, that being faith in Jesus Christ. They also bridged the gap between clergy and laypeople by insisting that it was the responsibility of all to know God in a real and personal way and by encouraging their followers to carry out ordinances and activities that had been traditionally reserved for an ordained clergy.

The preaching of Whitefield, Edwards, and others thus paved the way for nationhood. This is why Harvard professor, William Perry, said, "The Declaration of Independence of 1776 was a direct result of the evangelical preaching of the evangelists of the Great Awakening."[125]

Cultural Change

The Great Awakening literally changed the moral climate of colonial America. Entire communities were transformed. Profanity, lewdness, and drunkenness almost completely disappeared, especially in some areas. Reports in New England alone show thirty thousand to forty thousand converts and 150 new churches.

In addition, the revival spawned extensive missionary work and other humanitarian enterprises. Colleges such as Princeton, Columbia, and Hampden-Sydney were established to equip ministers for the new congregations. Kings College, now known as Columbia University, opened in 1754 with an advertisement in New York papers declaring,

> The chief thing in this college is to teach and engage children to know God in Jesus Christ and to love Him and serve Him in all sobriety, godliness, and richness of life with a perfect heart and willing mind."[126]

Hart points out that when Whitefield visited America for the final time in 1770, even the Episcopal (Anglican) churches, which had initially rejected him, opened their doors to him. He goes on to say,

> The true Spirit of Christ had dissolved sectarian differences. America considered itself to be a nation of Christians, pure and simple, as Whitefield noted with satisfaction. "Pulpits, hearts and affections," he said, were opened to him and any preacher of whatever denomination who had a true Christian message to share.[127]

No King but Jesus!
The War for Independence Begins

> If you ask an American who is his master,
> he will tell you he has none,
> nor any governor but Jesus Christ.
>
> *Jonathan Trumbull, British Appointed Governor*

In Ephesians 2:14, Paul wrote that Jesus Christ had broken down the dividing wall between Jew and Gentile. In a similar way, the Awakening's emphasis on faith in Jesus Christ as the central issue of Christianity, rather than church membership, gave the colonists a point of convergence in their various expressions of faith. This emphasis on the centrality of Christ broke down the doctrinal and denominational dividing walls so that a common cry would emerge in the conflict with Great Britain,

> "We recognize no Sovereign
> but God and no king but Jesus!"

The Tyranny of King George III

Even while the Awakening was impacting the American populace, relations with Great Britain were becoming increasingly strained. The imposition of burdensome taxes and regulations on the colonists without any input or representation on their part, provoked much anger and resentment.

King George III obviously looked upon the colonists as subjects rather than citizens and as a source of revenue for the British crown. The Sugar Act (1764), the Stamp Act (1765), the Townshend Act (1767) and other taxes and tariffs led to vehement protests throughout the colonies, but especially in New England. "No taxation without representation" became a common cry.

The colonists also detested the fact that the British crown had begun sending governors and setting up customs offices to look after its interests and enforce the taxes and regulations in the various colonies. With protests springing up, the British soon felt it necessary to send troops to the colonies to protect their people and interests, which only provoked further resentment.

The Boston Massacre

Tensions boiled over on March 5, 1770, when a group of Bostonians began pelting a security guard at a British customs office with snowballs and chunks of ice. Soldiers were called in to protect the guard and the office. When a scuffle broke out, the soldiers fired into the crowd, and when the smoke cleared, five Bostonians lay dead in the snow.

One of the fallen was a large black man of both African and Native American descent, named Crispus Attucks. When, in 1888, a monument was erected in memory of those who fell that day, a poem was recited honoring Attucks as "leader and voice that day; the first to defy and the first to die."[128]

Some modern historians have placed the blame for the massacre on the Colonists. Whatever the case, Samuel Adams used the incident to stir the passions of colonists in general, and Bostonians in particular, against the British control of the city.

No Bishops in America

The fears and frustrations of the colonists were further fueled when they heard that the Archbishop of Canterbury had sent a formal recommendation to the King that he begin appointing Anglican bishops in the colonies. This action was designed to bring the colonial churches into conformity with Church of England doctrine and polity. This proposal was vehemently opposed, even in Virginia where the Awakening had had a profound impact, moving the Anglican churches there closer to the Congregationalism of the Puritans and Baptists and further away from the High Church Anglicanism of England. One historian from that period wrote,

Those who belonged to the Church of England

were, for the most part, independents, as far as church government and hierarchy were concerned. They used the liturgy of that church, but were without bishops, and were strangers to those systems, which make religion an engine of the state.[129]

One must remember that it was the churches with episcopal/hierarchical forms of government, that is, churches ruled by bishops, that had commonly aligned themselves with the empire or state from the time of Constantine. The Radical Reformers had come to detest that form of church government and associated it with tyranny and oppression.

This is the context in which Jonathan Mayhew voiced vigorous opposition when he heard of this plan. A graduate of Harvard and pastor of Boston's West Church, Mayhew declared that such bishops would be mere extensions of the oppressive policies of King George, and he noted that, throughout history, bishops had been instruments for "establishing tyrannies over the bodies and souls of men."[130]

The Boston Tea Party

Things again reached a breaking point when the British Parliament imposed a tax on all tea in the Colonies, but left the British tea company—the East India Tea Company—free of the tax. It was obviously designed to put the American tea companies out of business and to rejuvenate the British company.

With emotions running high, a group of Bostonians decided to take matters into their own hands. Led by Samuel Adams and dressed as American Indians, about fifty patriots boarded three British ships anchored in Boston harbor loaded with tea from the East India Tea Company. Under the cover of darkness, they proceeded to relieve the ships of their cargo, dumping it all into the Boston Harbor. This became known as "The Boston Tea Party," and those patriots were applauded throughout the colonies for their act of bravery.

The Intolerable Acts

With these various protests erupting, especially in New England, King George III and Parliament decided to teach the upstart colonists a lesson with a series of laws that became known as the Intolerable Acts. These Acts closed the Boston seaport to all shipping and revoked the right of the people of Massachusetts to self-governance, something they had known since the days of the Pilgrims and Winthrop. Instead of officials being elected by the people, they were now to be appointed by the British Crown. Six regiments of British soldiers were assigned to occupy the city of Boston and enforce these "Intolerable Acts."

Throughout the colonies, from north to south, people identified with the people of Boston in their distress, and special days of prayer and fasting were appointed. In Virginia, for example, a resolution drafted by Thomas Jefferson was approved, appointing June 1 as a "day of fasting and prayer," and asking that all the oppressed people of America to "invoke the divine interposition to give the American people one heart and one mind to oppose all transgressions against American rights."[131]

With "foreign" troops now occupying one of their major cities, colonists in towns and villages began to look for ways to defend themselves. They, therefore, began forming militias and stockpiling weapons and ammunition. Samuel Adams, a Boston Puritan, formed the Sons of Liberty and held regular meetings in the Old South Church in Boston to discuss how to deal with the British "occupation." He also organized the Committees of Correspondence, which disseminated information and provided networking for the scattered patriots throughout the different colonies.

The Role of Ministers

Pastors and evangelists played a vital role in these proceedings by giving the people a theological justification for resisting King George with force of arms. To accomplish this, they drew on the radical Protestant tradition of the Separatist Puritans, Baptists and Quakers who had come to America because of a refusal to conform to the unjust and unethical demands of monarchs and bishops.

In their fiery sermons, colonial preachers proclaimed God as the God of liberty who desires freedom for his people. They drew heavily on the Old Testament image of God delivering Israel from Egypt's bondage and many saw themselves as a sort of new Israel and King George as a modern Pharaoh. They also emphasized Biblical passages such as Acts 5:29, where, in response to the demand of the Jewish authorities that they cease speaking in the name of Jesus, the apostles declared, *We ought to obey God rather than men.*

When someone pointed to Romans 13:1-4, which calls for subjection to the governing authorities and refers to the government official as a *minister of God,* Mayhew stepped forward once again and pointed out that the passage refers to just and benevolent rulers, not tyrants. In strong language he declared, "It is blasphemy to call tyrants and oppressors God's ministers."[132]

Far from war mongering, the colonial preachers emphasized that a just war could only be a war of self-defense and only entered into once all other avenues for peace had been exhausted. Speaking to an educated and informed populace, the ministers found it necessary to answer every argument and question. For example, regarding Jesus' words about turning the other cheek, they explained that this was related to personal matters when one suffers for their faith, but in civil matters, where an entire people is being threatened, civil government has a responsibility before God to act on behalf of its citizens.

The Colonial preachers succeeded in convincing the populace that theirs was a just cause and that God would vindicate them and fight for them. This is why John Wingate Thornton wrote, "To the Pulpit, the Puritan Pulpit, we owe the moral force which won our independence."[133] Hart agrees and writes,

> The major reason these men took up the fight against the great British empire was their steadfast

belief that they were an intricate part of God's plan. Religious conviction gave them the strength needed to persevere in the seven-year war for American independence.[134]

The Beginning
of the War for Independence

On April 18, 1775, John Adams and John Hancock, prominent New England leaders in the protests, were at the home of Rev. Jonas Clarke in the area of Lexington, about fifteen miles from Boston. Lexington had become a center of protest, with the people forming a militia and creating an ammunition depot in nearby Concord.

General Gage, the British general stationed in Boston, heard of these activities and decided to put an end to the rebellion. That same night, April 18, Gage sent out a detachment of about eight hundred soldiers, hoping to take the colonists by surprise, arrest Adams and Hancock, and capture the ammunition depot.

Also, that same night, Paul Revere made his famous ride through the countryside from Boston to Lexington. As he rode, he shouted along the way, "The Redcoats are coming!" This deprived the British of their element of surprise.

When the British arrived at Lexington, the local militia, made up mostly of farmers known as "Minutemen," were ready and waiting. They were told to lay down their arms and all but Samuel Adams and John Hancock would be forgiven. The Minutemen, however, refused to yield.

The Minutemen were determined not to fire first, so as not to be the aggressors. During the standoff, however, a shot rang out and both sides began firing. Later, both sides claimed that the other side fired the first shot. Nonetheless, when the smoke cleared, nine Minutemen lay dead and ten more were seriously wounded. A wife of one of the Minutemen was seen sobbing over her husband's body.

Major Pitcairn, who was commanding the British forces, was convinced that he had everything under control as he now marched toward Concord to take possession of the depot of ammunition. However, word spread of what had happened, and patriots began to rush to the aid of the Minutemen from throughout the region so that, when Pitcairn and his troops reached Concord, they were met by a large number of patriots, whose ranks continued to swell.

After destroying most of the ammunition depot, Pitcairn ordered a withdrawal and began a retreat to Boston. The Americans, however, fired on the retreating British, who fired back. The patriots had learned to fight in the manner of the local natives, and knowing the terrain, they were able to take shortcuts and ambush the retreating British from behind trees, stone walls, barns, and from wherever they could find cover.

The patriots harassed the British all the way back to Boston. At times, the British soldiers panicked, with some throwing away their weapons as they sought to outrun the patriots. In all, the British casualties included 65 dead and 180 wounded, while the Colonist casualties included 50 dead and 38 wounded or missing.[135] The first shot fired in Lexington became known as "the shot heard round the world," and it marked the beginning of the Revolutionary War (1775-1783).

No King but Jesus

Before the first shot was fired in Lexington, Rev. Clarke made a strategic declaration. It was a spontaneous response to Major Pitcairn's demand to the Minutemen, "Disperse, ye villains, lay down your arms in the name of George the Sovereign King of England." Rev. Clarke shouted, "We recognize no Sovereign but God and no king but Jesus!"[136]

That cry caught the imagination of American patriots everywhere, and soon it was heard throughout the colonies. In fact, when a British-appointed governor, Jonathan Trumbull, wrote to England, he said, "If you ask an American who is his master, he will tell you he has none, nor any governor but Jesus Christ."[137]

Chapter 10

A Nation Birthed in Prayer

In all moments of imminent danger,
as in the first Act of the First Continental Congress,
the founding generation turned to prayer.

Michael Novak, Historian

Even before fighting broke out in April of 1775 in Lexington and Concord, it was obvious to most Americans that drastic measures must be taken in response to the oppressive tactics of King George. With anger and tensions rising throughout the colonies, and sometimes boiling over, a call went forth for a gathering of delegates from the Thirteen Colonies to coordinate a unified response to the British oppression. These delegates, in what became known as the First Continental Congress, met for the first time at Carpenter's Hall in Philadelphia on September 5, 1774.

As delegates traveled from New England in the north, and from as far south as South Carolina, it weighed heavily on their minds and hearts how regiments of British troops had occupied the city of Boston and closed its port, and how British ships had shelled the port city of Charleston in the south.

The First Continental Congress
Opens with Prayer

This Congress would not have been possible apart from the Great Awakening, which had broken down social and denominational barriers. This became obvious at the first meeting on September 5, 1774, when it was proposed that they begin their deliberations with prayer. Two delegates opposed the motion on the grounds that they were such a diverse religious group, including Anglicans, Puritans, Presbyterians and Quakers, that it would be impossible for them to pray together.

Samuel Adams, a Puritan from Boston who had been impacted by the Awakening, arose and said that he was not a bigoted man and that he could join in prayer with any person of piety and virtue who loved his country. He went on to say that, although he was a stranger to Philadelphia, he had heard of an Anglican minister, a Rev. Jacob Dusche, who was such a man, and he proposed that they invite him to come and lead them in prayer. Adams' proposal was approved and Dusche was asked to preside over a time of Bible reading and prayer.

As the elderly, grey-haired Dusche stood before the Congress, he began by reading the entire 35th Psalm, which powerfully impacted everyone present. It is a prayer of David for deliverance and begins with the words, *Plead my cause O LORD with those who strive against me; fight against those who fight against me.* The Psalm ends with praise for God's deliverance.

As the Psalm was read, a unique sense of God's presence filled the room and tears flowed from many eyes. John Adams wrote to his wife, Abigail, of the impact of the Bible reading and prayer on the delegates. He wrote,

> Who can realize the emotions with which they turned imploringly to heaven for divine interposition and aid. It was enough to melt a heart of stone. I never saw a greater effect upon an audience. It seems as if heaven had ordained that Psalm to be read that day. I saw tears gush into the eyes of the old, grave pacific Quakers of Philadelphia. I must beg you to read that Psalm.[138]

After reading the Psalm, Dusche began praying for the delegates, for America, and especially for the city of Boston and its inhabitants who were under siege. As he began praying, the Anglicans, such as George Washington and Richard Henry Lee, knelt in prayer, according to their custom. The Puritans, according to their custom, sat with bowed heads and prayed. Others prayed according to their own, unique customs. But although their outward manners differed, there was a singleness of heart and purpose as they all united in prayer for God's assistance and intervention for America.

The Congress and the Nation Prays

Prayer continued to be a daily and vital part of the proceedings of the Continental Congresses. Indeed, the Catholic scholar, Michael Novak, is correct when he says, "In all moments of imminent danger, as in the first Act of the First Continental Congress, the founding generation turned to prayer."[139]

During the Revolutionary War, the Congress issued no less than fifteen separate calls for special days of prayer and fasting. For example, during the fall of 1776, when the morale of the army and populace had sunk to an all-time low because of a poor harvest and hardship on the battlefield, Congress proclaimed December 11, 1776, as a Day of Fasting and Repentance.

Jonathan Witherspoon, a Presbyterian Reformer and member of the Congress, was deputized to write the proclamation, which was then approved by the rest of the Congress. It reads, in part,

> WHEREAS, the war in which the United States are engaged with Great Britain, has not only been prolonged, but is likely to be carried to the greatest extremity; and whence it becomes all public bodies, as well as private persons, to reverence the Providence of God, and look up to him as the supreme disposer of all events, and the arbiter of the fate of nations; therefore; RESOLVED, That it be recommended to all the United States, as soon as possible, to appoint a day of solemn fasting and humiliation; to implore of Almighty God the forgiveness of the many sins prevailing among all ranks, and to beg the assistance of his Providence in the prosecution of the present just and necessary war. The Congress do also, in the most earnest manner, recommend to the members of the United States, and particularly the officers civil and

military under them, the exercise of repentance and reformation, and the strict observance of the articles of war, particularly that part which forbids profane swearing and all immorality, of which all such officers are desired to take notice.[140]

There was an amazing change of circumstances after this day of prayer, with successes on the battlefield and the reaping of abundant harvests. There was, in fact, such a turnaround after this that in 1779 Congress issued a proclamation setting aside a day of thanksgiving, because "it hath pleased Almighty God, the father of mercies, remarkably to assist and support the United States of America in their important struggle for liberty."

The Congress then listed seven different accomplishments of God on the behalf of the nation, including "many instances of prowess and success in our armies" and "so great abundance of the fruits of the earth of every kind, as not only to enable us to easily to supply the wants of the army, but gives comfort and happiness to the whole people."[141]

The Miracle at Long Island

One of the answers to prayer recounted by Congress was the deliverance of the Colonial army from certain defeat while quartered on Long Island's western end. The British Generals Howe, Clinton, and Cornwallis, seeing an opportunity to trap the 12,000-member Colonial force, moved an army at least twice that size behind them and took up positions to march forward and trap them against the East River. Confident that they would put a quick end to the rebellion, the British retired for the night, planning to begin their offensive in the morning.

In the meantime, Washington, seeing the predicament they were in, sent out a desperate call for every available vessel. Under cover of darkness, they began to evacuate troops and equipment across the East River to Manhattan.

Throughout the night, the Colonial soldiers secured boats, marched in silence, rowed, and prayed. But as dawn approached, it was obvious that they were far from their objective, with only a fraction of their troops and equipment having been moved. It looked as though they were about to lose everything.

But just before dawn, as if in answer to their prayers, fog rolled in. It was a heavy fog, the kind that allows a person to see for only a few feet ahead. Under cover of this shroud, the Colonists continued marching, rowing, and praying. By noon, the entire army, with their cannons and other armaments, had been moved to Manhattan. And then the fog lifted.

At this point, the British were amazed to see that the Colonial army had disappeared, as if into thin air. Every American had escaped with every piece of cannon and armament. It was truly a miracle. Novak, says,

> Many thanks to God went heavenward. For many men the miracle of Long Island was one of those "signal interventions" of Divine Providence of which both Washington and the author of *Federalist 37* made mention.[142]

Washington Chosen
to Lead the Colonial Army

The Second Continental Congress, which convened on May 10, 1775, asked George Washington to become commander-in-chief of the ragtag Colonial militias and to transform them into an army that could face the mighty British war machine. Washington accepted the call, and immediately, he set out to instill in the troops a moral and spiritual discipline, as well as a faith in God and the American cause.

Washington was chosen because he had gained recognition for his leadership ability and courage in battle, first of all, as an aide to General Braddock in his ill-fated attack on Fort Duquesne (present day Pittsburg) during the French and Indian Wars. Washington, still in his early 20s at the time, had been recruited by the British because of his knowledge of the ways of both the wilderness and the Indians. Both of these, he had acquired in his work as a surveyor of wilderness territory.

Braddock ignored Washington's advice about traveling through the wilderness and about dealing with the Natives. However, when they were ambushed by about one thousand Native Americans and their French allies, and Braddock himself was wounded, Washington took charge. Amidst the war whoops of the attackers and the cries of the wounded and dying, Washington rode back and forth through the hail of bullets, shouting orders and directing an orderly retreat.

It was a blood bath for the British forces. Of the 1,459

soldiers, 977 were killed or wounded. Putting his own life at risk, Washington rescued hundreds of the wounded and dying, placing them in wagons. During the chaos, two horses were shot out from under him and his clothes were shredded with bullets. Miraculously, perhaps, Washington emerged unscathed and gave glory to God, saying, "I was saved by the miraculous care of providence that saved me beyond human expectation."

From that time forward, Washington's reputation for bravery spread among both the English and the Native Americans. In fact, fifteen years later, in 1770, he had an amazing encounter with one of the Native American chiefs who fought that day on the side of the French.

According to historian George Bancroft, Washington and a friend were exploring an area along the Ohio River when they encountered a group of Native Americans. Recognizing Washington, the Natives invited the men back to their camp to meet with their Chief, whom it turned out, had fought on the side of the French in the Battle of Duquesne. They had a cordial visit and then the old Chief, pointing to Washington, spoke an amazing prophecy. He said,

> I am chief and ruler over all my tribes. My influence extends to the waters of the Great Lakes, and to the far blue mountains. I have traveled a long and weary path that I might see the young warrior of the great battle. It was on the day when the white man's blood mixed with the streams of our forest that I first beheld this chief. I called to my young men and said, 'Mark yon tall and daring

warrior? He is not of the redcoat tribe—he hath an Indian's wisdom, and his warriors fight as we do—himself alone is exposed. Quick, let your aim be certain, and he dies.' Our rifles were leveled—rifles which, but for him, knew not how to miss. 'Twas all in vain; a power far mightier than we shielded him from harm. He cannot die in battle. The Great Spirit protects that man, and guides his destinies. He will become chief of nations, and a people yet unborn will hail him the founder of a mighty nation.[143]

Prayer and the Revolutionary Army

Washington accepted the call of the Congress and began immediately to instill in the Colonial troops a very real faith in God, for as Novak says,

> Washington knew his only hope lay in a profound conviction in the hearts and daily actions of all his men that what they did they did for God, and under God's protection.[144]

Washington, therefore, issued an order that each day was to begin with prayer led by the officers of each unit. He also ordered that, unless their duties required them to be elsewhere, every soldier was to observe, "a punctual attendance of Divine services, to implore the blessing of heaven upon the means used for our safety and public defense." He also forbade all profanity and promised swift punishment for any who uttered oaths that would offend God or man.

Washington continually sought to instill in his troops

faith and reverence toward God. While quartering at Valley Forge, during a particularly difficult part of the war, Rev. Henry Muhlenberg was able to observe Washington's conduct from his nearby Lutheran Church. He wrote, "Washington rode around among his army yesterday and admonished each one to fear God."[145]

That Washington himself was a devout person in his private life was confirmed by Isaac Potts, a Quaker who lived near Valley Forge, Pennsylvania, when the Continental Army, led by Washington, was wintering there under much duress in 1774-75. Potts was a pacifist who opposed the war until he had a life-changing experience while riding through the woods one day during, perhaps, the bleakest period of the war. He said,

> I heard a plaintive sound as of a man at prayer. I tied my horse to a sapling and went quietly into the woods and to my astonishment I saw the great George Washington on his knees alone, with his sword on one side and his cocked hat on the other. He was at Prayer to the God of the Armies, beseeching to interpose with his Divine aid, as it was ye Crisis, and the cause of the country, of humanity and of the world. Such a prayer I never heard from the lips of man. I left him alone praying. I went home and told my wife I saw a sight and heard today what I never saw or heard before, and just related to her what I had seen and heard and observed. We never thought a man could be a soldier and a Christian, but if there is one in the world, it is Washington.[146]

The Declaration of Independence

After much prayer, discussion, and debate, the delegates of the Continental Congress, decided that it was time to declare the independence of the American colonies. Thomas Jefferson was chosen to draft the document, and a select committee of five, including Benjamin Franklin, was chosen to assist in its formulation. It was publicly read for the first time on July 4, 1776.

This founding document anchors individual rights, not in any human institution or government, but in God.

We hold these truths to be self-evident that all men [people] are created equal and are endowed by their Creator with certain inalienable rights such as life, liberty and the pursuit of happiness.

Jefferson, Franklin, and the other Founders saw human rights as having a transcendent source, that being, God Himself. They and their forebears had suffered the loss of their rights and their being given or taken at the whim of a monarch, pope, or bishop. In this new nation, they were determined to fix them in a place beyond human reach. Government, they insisted, did not exist to give or take away rights, but to protect those rights already given by God.

Three names for God drawn directly from the Judeo-Christian tradition were used in the Declaration. They "Creator," "Supreme Judge," and "Divine Providence." They did not use Christian, redemptive words in the document, such as "Savior" or "Redeemer," for they were aware that they were formulating, not a statement of faith for a church, but the founding document for a nation.

The use of these names for God confirms what is expressed in so many ways by the Founders; namely, that they considered belief in God as Creator and Judge to be essential for good citizenship. Unless the citizens would have a moral sense of obligation to their Creator, they would tend to live self-centered lives, harmful to society. This is why James Madison wrote,

> The belief in a God All Powerful wise and good, is so essential to the moral order of the world and to the happiness of man, that arguments which enforce it cannot be drawn from too many sources nor adapted with too much solicitude to the different characters and capacities impressed with it.[147]

The use of the word "Providence" is especially interesting, for it was commonly used as a synonym for the God of the Bible in the 18th century, even by ministers. It was not a generic, impersonal reference to deity as some have suggested. Even a fiery revivalist such as Whitefield often used it in referring to God.

"Providence" was a word that expressed faith in God as the One who is superintending the course of history and overruling, even the actions of evil men, in order to bring about His plan and purpose. This is why Roger Williams, after being banished from Massachusetts by the Puritans in 1636, and making his way in the winter to Rhode Island, founded a city there, which he named "Providence." This expressed his faith that God would overrule the wrong that he believed had been done to him and would bring about His plan for his life.

131

The only clergyman to sign the Declaration, Jonathan Witherspoon, preached a sermon entitled "The Dominion of Providence over the Passions of Men," less than two months before signing the document along with the others. Witherspoon was a Presbyterian minister and president of the College of New Jersey, now Princeton University. In this sermon on Providence, he emphasized the necessity of believing that God would bring good out of the evil situation of the day; that is, that the ambition of mistaken princes and the cruelty of oppressive rulers would finally promote the glory of God. This is Providence.

The final paragraph of the Declaration shows that this was the faith of the Founders, for in it, they express their trust in God for His providential protection and support in their momentous act. It reads,

> And for the support of this declaration, with a firm reliance on the protection of Divine Providence, we mutually pledge to each other our Lives, our Fortunes, and our sacred Honor.

After the signing of the document and knowing that King George III would view their actions as treason, John Hancock exhorted, "We must all hang together." Franklin is said to have quipped, "Yes, if do not all hang together, we will surely all hang separately."

Independence is Obtained

The Revolutionary War lasted for seven years. It was a costly war, especially for the fifty-six signers of the

Declaration of Independence. Of the fifty-six who signed the Declaration, nine died of wounds or hardships during the war. Five were captured and imprisoned, in each case, enduring brutal treatment. Several lost wives, sons, or entire families. One lost his thirteen children. Two wives were brutally treated. All were, at one time or another, the victims of manhunts and were driven from their homes. Twelve signers had their homes completely burned. Seventeen lost everything they owned. Yet not one defected or went back on his pledged word.[148]

The war officially came to an end on October 19, 1781, when General Cornwallis surrendered his entire force to Washington. In customary fashion, Cornwallis turned his sword over to Washington, and the weaponry of his troops was stacked in neat piles. As this occurred the British band played, "The World Turned Upside Down." For freedom-loving people everywhere, however, the world had been turned right side up.

Showing the influence of Christianity on the American populace and their leaders, there was none of the revenge and butchery that are so common in Marxist and Islamic revolutions. There were no tribunals to exact revenge, no reign of terror, and no bloodthirsty proclamations by the Continental Congress. The war ended and the patriots picked up their lives and moved on.

Having completed his call, Washington issued a letter of resignation as Commander-In-Chief to the Continental Congress. Then, he wrote what could be described as a pastoral letter, dated June 14, 1783, to the governors of the various states. This letter included his "earnest prayer" that is here quoted in part. He wrote,

> I now make it my earnest prayer that God would have you, and the State over which you preside, in his holy protection; that he would incline the hearts of the citizens . . . to entertain a brotherly affection and love for one another . . . and to demean ourselves with that charity, humility, and pacific temper of mind, which were the characteristics of the Divine Author of our blessed religion, and without a humble imitation of His example in these things, we can never hope to be a happy nation.[149]

Our Response

Seeing the vital role of prayer in the birthing of this nation, let us not be intimidated by the assertion that prayer is somehow inappropriate for public or political venues. Let us be bold in our faith. Let us be salt and light in this generation. Let us pray. It is the godly thing to do! It is the American thing to do!

ॐॐ Chapter 11 ॐॐ

The Faith of the Founders

> It cannot be emphasized too strongly or too often
> that this great nation was founded,
> not by religionists, but by Christians;
> not on religions,
> but on the gospel of Jesus Christ.
>
> *Patrick Henry, Founding Father*

There is no question that most, if not all, of the Founding Fathers were impacted by the Great Awakening. We have already seen how Benjamin Franklin was directly impacted by the Awakening. Benjamin Rush, a signer of the Declaration of Independence and a central figure at the Continental Congress, attributed the development of his thinking and ideals to the preachers of the Great Awakening. [150] Amos and Gardiner correctly state:

> The majority of people who founded the United States of America either experienced, or were children of those who experienced, the religious awakening of the 1740s. [151]

This meant that the Christianity of the Founders, for the most part, was not a dry, formal, orthodoxy based on

135

church membership, but instead, was a vital faith that was both known in the head and experienced in the heart. As Patrick Henry so eloquently declared,

> It cannot be emphasized too strongly or too often that this great nation was founded, not by religionists, but by Christians; not on religions, but on the gospel of Jesus Christ.[152]

On the following pages, the faith of six of the Founders is highlighted. Four were chosen because of their significance, and two—John Witherspoon and Charles Carrol—were chosen because they are so little known to the average American. Franklin and Jefferson are included, not only for their significance, but to dispel popular notions concerning their alleged anti-Christian secularism.

George Washington (1732-1799)

George Washington was born in Westmoreland County, Virginia, in 1732, to Augustine Washington and his wife, Mary Ball Washington. His father died when Washington was eleven years old, which meant he developed a sense of responsibility at an early age.

Washington's mother was a devout Christian who sought to raise her son as a committed believer in Christ. Just before he left home as a young soldier, she admonished him, "Remember that God is our only sure trust." She also exhorted, "My son, neglect not the duty of secret prayer."[153]

That Washington was influenced by the Great Awakening

seems likely because of the personal piety that was such an integral part of his life. It seems likely, as well, because of the impact the Awakening had on his home state of Virginia while he was still a lad. This would help explain his deep, sincere faith, for as Charles Hodge said, "In no part of our country was the revival more interesting, and in very few was it so pure as in Virginia"[154]

The impact of the Awakening and his mother's influence set the spiritual tone, no doubt, for his life. A prayer journal has been discovered that Washington kept when he was in his twenties. He called it *Daily Sacrifice.* The first entry reads in part,

> Let my heart, therefore, gracious God, be so affected with the glory and majesty of Thine honor that I may not do my own works, but wait on Thee, and discharge those duties which Thou requirest of me.[155]

The following Monday morning, his prayer reads,

> Direct my thoughts, words and work, wash away my sins in the immaculate blood of the Lamb, and purge my heart by Thy Holy Spirit . . . daily frame me more and more in the likeness of Thy Son Jesus Christ.[156]

Washington took the oath of office with his hand placed on a Bible. This was no mere political formality, for he had once declared, "It is impossible to rightly govern the world without God and the Bible."[157] This act, which has become a tradition for succeeding presidents, signified the Founders' belief that the oath of office is a sacred act in which the president promises to uphold and defend the Constitution.

After his inaugural address, which was filled with references to God and the Bible, Washington and the Congress proceeded to St. Paul's chapel to participate in a worship service.[158] Washington also once publicly prayed, "Bless, O Lord, the whole race of mankind, and let the world be filled with the knowledge of Thee and Thy Son, Jesus Christ."[159]

It was his faith that nurtured in Washington the qualities and character that would be needed in his vital role in America's origins. That he was no mere politician was revealed when he was a young man serving as commander-in-chief of the Virginia militias with ultimate responsibility for the safety of the populace. While headquartered in Winchester, terrifying reports of Indian raids on frontier settlements came to him, telling of burnings, scalpings and death.

As Washington read the reports and the desperate pleas for help, he was overwhelmed with grief and with compassion for the suffering. From what could be called a caring, pastoral heart, willing to sacrifice his own life for sake of others, he wrote,

> The supplications and the tears melt me into such deadly sorrow that I solemnly declare, if I know my own mind, I would offer myself a sacrifice to the butchering enemy, provided that would contribute to the people's ease. I would be a willing offering to savage fury, and die by inches to save a people.[160]

It was this sort of selfless service that endeared Washington to the hearts of early Americans who considered him "The Father of His Country." Although he wanted to retire to his Mt. Vernon home at the end of the War, the other Founders convinced him that he was the only one with the respect necessary to guide the nation in its formative years. Washington conceded and was unanimously elected, not once, but twice, to the presidential office.

First in war; first in peace;
and first in the hearts of his countrymen.

This was an apt adage that the founding generation gave to George Washington.

Benjamin Franklin (1706-1790)

Benjamin Franklin is often considered one of the least religious of the Founding Fathers. In his early years, he did entertain Deistic views about God and the Bible. However, his religious sentiments and views changed through the years, attributable, no doubt, to his Puritan roots, his exposure to the Great Awakening, and his friendship with George Whitefield.

Franklin was born into a Puritan home in Boston and the evidence suggests that his forebears were Separatist Puritans on both sides of the family. He refers to them as "dissenting Protestants" and tells how his father, Josiah Franklin, fled England in 1685, with his first wife and three small children, in order to escape religious persecution. In his *Autobiography*, Franklin says they came under persecution in England because of their attendance at "conventicles," which were religious

139

gatherings that had been outlawed by the British government. [161]

A voracious reader as a child, he was exposed to Deism by reading religious treatises against it. He later read books by Deists, and by the age of seventeen had decided that he was a Deist. However, by the time George Whitefield and the Awakening came to Philadelphia in 1739, Franklin had already moved away from Deism, deciding that it did not provide motivation for the ethical and moral behavior necessary for a stable society.[162]

Franklin embraced both Whitfield and the Awakening. He and Whitefield became close friends and business partners, with Franklin taking on the task of printing and selling Whitefield's sermons and journals. He also advised Whitefield in business matters, including Whitefield's vision for an orphanage in Georgia.

In his *Autobiography*, Franklin refers to Whitefield as "a perfectly honest man," and he describes their friendship as being "sincere on both sides, which lasted till his death."[163] Whitefield stayed in Franklin's home while visiting Philadelphia, and it is obvious that, in spite of their differences, their friendship ran deep. Franklin wrote to his brother James, a printer in Boston, saying, "Whitefield is a good man and I love him."[164]

Also, in his *Autobiography*, written a number of years after Whitefield's death, Franklin says that Whitefield often prayed for his conversion but did not live to see his prayers answered. By that statement, does Franklin imply that Whitefield's prayers for his conversion were answered after his death? Although that question may be debatable, what is not debatable is that Whitefield's influence moved Franklin back toward his Puritan roots of faith and freedom.

This became obvious just a few years after Whitefield's initial visit at a time when many in Philadelphia had become concerned about their safety due to the fact that Britain was at war with Spain. Although the region was a British colony, there were no British soldiers to protect them from marauding Spanish ships that might attack.

Franklin, therefore, led the way in organizing a citizen's militia and in building fortifications with cannons posted at the edge of the city. Then, he proposed that the Assembly and civic leaders issue a call for a day of prayer and fasting, "to implore the blessing of Heaven on our undertaking."

The people of Philadelphia had no knowledge of such a practice, but Franklin was able to draw on his Puritan roots in New England, where public days of prayer and fasting had been observed since the time the Pilgrims landing at Plymouth in 1620. He wrote,

> They embraced the motion; but as it was the first fast ever thought of in the province, the secretary had no precedent from which to draw the proclamation. My education in New England, where a fast is proclaimed every year, was here of some advantage. I drew it in the accustomed style, it was translated into German, printed in both languages, and divulged through the province.[165]

Franklin and all of Pennsylvania, including government

officials, subsequently participated in a day of prayer and fasting, imploring God's blessing and protection on their colony. Even at this early stage of his life, he obviously saw no conflict between God, prayer, and government. Indeed, throughout his life, Franklin would consider Christian values a necessary force for a prosperous and stable society.

His commitment to Christian values for a stable society was borne out when the well-known Deist, Thomas Paine, sent him a manuscript copy of a book he had written challenging the idea of a providential God and other aspects of orthodox Christianity. Franklin refused to print the book, and in very strong language, he urged Paine not even to allow anyone else to see it. He wrote,

> I would advise you, therefore . . . to burn this piece before it is seen by any other person; whereby you will save yourself a great deal of mortification by the enemies it may raise against you, and perhaps a good deal of regret and repentance. If men are so wicked with religion [Christianity], what would they be if without it.[166]

Although Franklin stopped attending the Presbyterian Church in Philadelphia over a disagreement concerning the dismissal of a pastor he liked, he heartily attended other meetings, such as those of Whitefield. And when he learned that his daughter had stopped attending church because of a personal dislike of the minister, Franklin wrote her a letter in which he exhorted her on "the necessity and duty of attending church."[167] In regards to her not liking the minister, Franklin, with typical wit, reminded her, "Pure water is often found to have come through very dirty earth.[168]

Franklin was an avid reader of the Bible and would often quote Scripture in his writings and conversations. He also kept certain Christian events and festivals. This was made obvious when he told of being a vegetarian for a time and how it positively affected his health. He then commented that he celebrated Lent by going back to his vegetarian diet. He wrote, "I have since kept several Lents most strictly, leaving the common diet for that."[169]

After a voyage to England in 1757, during which the ship almost crashed at midnight into a small rocky island in the Atlantic, Franklin wrote a letter to his wife, in which he said,

> The bell ringing for church, we went thither immediately, and with hearts full of gratitude, returned sincere thanks to God for the mercies we had received. If I were a Roman Catholic, perhaps I should, on this occasion, vow to build a chapel to some saint; but as I am not, if I were to vow at all, it should be to build a light house.[170]

On June 28, 1787, seventeen years after the death of Whitefield, the Constitutional Convention was about to be suspended because of unresolved dissension. It was a critical moment! Franklin, now 81 years of age, rose to his feet and addressed George Washington, the Convention's President, with these words:

> How has it happened, sir, that we have not hitherto once thought of humbly appealing to the Father of

lights to illuminate our understandings? In the beginning of the contest with Great Britain, when we were sensible to danger, we had daily prayers in this room for Divine protection. Our prayers, sir, were heard and they were graciously answered. I have lived, sir, a long time and the longer I live, the more convincing proofs I see of this truth—that God governs in the affairs of men. And if a sparrow cannot fall to the ground without his notice, is it probable that an empire can rise without His aid? We have been assured, sir, in the sacred writings that *except the Lord build the house, they labor in vain that build it*. I firmly believe this. I therefore beg leave to move that, henceforth, prayers imploring the assistance of heaven and its blessing on our deliberation be held in this assembly every morning before we proceed to business.[171]

The notion that Franklin was a Deist who would not want faith in God to be a part of public proceedings is based on either a lack of knowledge or a distortion of the facts. Franklin, like the other Founders, believed Christian morality to be absolutely necessary for a stable and prosperous society.

James Madison (1751-1836)

James Madison is best known as the chief architect of the Constitution and the fourth president of the United States. He was a devout Christian and he was trained in the College of New Jersey, formerly the Log College, which was a center of religious activity during the Great

Awakening. There, he had been mentored by Jonathan Witherspoon, who was the school's president and a Presbyterian Reformer who had suffered incarceration in England because of his faith.

That Madison was a devout follower of Jesus is obvious from his many public and private writings. For example, in a letter to his friend, William Bradford, Madison exhorted him to make sure of his own salvation, saying,

> A watchful eye must be kept on ourselves lest, while we are building ideal monuments of renown and bliss here, we neglect to have our names enrolled in the Annals of Heaven."[172]

He also expressed to this same friend his desire that public officials would openly testify of their faith in Christ, and encouraged him to do so. He wrote,

> I have sometimes thought there could not be a stronger testimony in favor of religion than for men who occupy the most honorable and gainful departments . . . becoming fervent advocates in the cause of Christ; and I wish you may give your evidence in this way.[173]

When he served as President, Madison signed a federal bill in 1812 that provided economic aid for a Bible society in its goal of the mass distribution of the Bible. And throughout his presidency (1809-1816), Madison issued several proclamations for national days of prayer, fasting and thanksgiving.

This should not be surprising, for much of Madison's

education occurred in overt Christian settings. At age sixteen, he began a two-year course of study with Reverend Thomas Martin to prepare himself for college. Following this, he enrolled in the College of New Jersey, which was a center of Spiritual Awakening leading up to the time of the Revolution.

As a Virginian, Madison was expected to attend the College at William and Mary, but instead, he chose to attend the College of New Jersey, probably because of its strong Christian stance and the reputation of its president, John Witherspoon, who had been trained at Cambridge University in England. Witherspoon became an adviser and teacher to many of the founding fathers, and a signer of the Declaration of Independence. Madison became his most famous student.

After his graduation, Madison continued at the College of New Jersey for another year, where he translated the Bible from Hebrew and Greek into English. Madison's worldview was thereby shaped by associates and institutions firmly rooted in the Great Awakening. This is why Dr. D. James Kennedy and Jerry Newcombe said, "Madison's political worldview was one shaped by the Bible more than any other source."[174]

In 1946, a body of Madison's writings from later in life, which he never made public, was discovered in which he questions government proclamations of prayer and chaplains in the military. This "Detached Memoranda," as it has been called, has been seized upon by secularists who seek to use it to assert that Madison was against faith being expressed in the public and political arenas.

It is obvious, however, that Madison was concerned, not about the effect religion would have on government, but about the negative effect government would have on religion. Having been trained in Christian history from the perspective of the Protestant Reformers, Madison was aware of the distinct and specific roles the Reformers had assigned to the church and to civil government. This had become known at the "Creator-Redeemer Distinction."

In response to the church and state being merged by Constantine and to the ensuing corruption of the church, the Reformers emphasized that God rules over two separate realms, those being the natural and the spiritual. All citizens, whether Christian or non-Christian, have a responsibility to relate to God as Creator in the natural or civil realm. Christians, however, relate to God, not only as Creator, but also as Redeemer. And this is where the Reformers drew the line. They said that the civil government should have no role in the church or in the life of the individual Christian. How a person related to God as Redeemer, they stated, was outside the jurisdiction of the civil government. This was the "Creator-Redeemer Distinction."

Some of the Radical Reformers argued that the church should not accept any offer of support or sanction from the civil government. Any church that becomes beholden to the government, they argued, loses its ability to be a corrective voice to that government, because it has put itself in the precarious position of being dependent on that government for its security and well-being.

With Christianity being such a cultural force in American

society, Madison was also concerned to maintain religious liberty for all. This is clearly borne out in his comments in this "Detached Memoranda" on a failed attempt to include the words "Jesus Christ" in the preamble of a religious freedom bill in the Virginia state legislature. Madison was concerned that, by including the name of the "Savior" in a bill guaranteeing religious liberty, non-Christians would be discriminated against. He says,

> The opponents of the amendment turned the judgment of the House against it, by successfully contending that the better proof of reverence for that Holy Name would be not to profane it by making it a topic of legislative discussion and particularly by making His religion the means of abridging the rights of other men, in defiance of His own declaration that His kingdom was not of this world.[175]

These were the sorts of issues and questions that would have been discussed when Madison was at the College of New Jersey under the tutelage of John Witherspoon. So Madison obviously raised these questions here as one who wanted to protect both individual liberty and the purity of Christianity. That this was his concern is spelled out in a statement in 1822 to Edward Livingston. He wrote,

> We are teaching the world a great truth, that governments do better without kings and nobles than with them. The merit will be doubled by the other lesson: that Religion flourishes in greater

purity without, than with the aid of government."[176]

Thomas Jefferson (1743-1826)

Thomas Jefferson, along with Franklin, is often pointed to by secularists as one of the non-Christian founders of this nation, the champion of the separation of church and state, and an advocate for keeping religion out of government. Nothing could be further from the truth!

Jefferson was a life-long member of the Anglican Church, and he worked tirelessly for religious freedom as Governor of Virginia, and later, as the third President of the United States. As both Governor and President, he used his position to advance Christian causes.

Although Jefferson, in the latter part of his life, expressed personal doubts about the Trinity and the deity of Christ, the impact of Christianity and the Great Awakening on his thinking is obvious. Jefferson was educated in Christian schools and regularly attended church throughout his life. As the Governor of Virginia, he worked closely with the Baptists to change the laws of Virginia that had made the Church of England the official church and by which the Baptists and other Christian groups were persecuted and marginalized.

In spite of the doubts he expressed in later life—probably prompted by the tragic losses of his wife, his mother, and a friend—he was thoroughly Christian in his thinking and held to a Christian world-view. He never considered himself a Deist, and he said, "I am a real Christian, that is to say, a disciple of the doctrines of

Jesus."[177] His actions clearly demonstrate that he welcomed Christian influence in the public and political arenas and that he saw no problem with the government advancing Christian causes.

For example, as President, Jefferson sat on the front row of church services that were held each Sunday in one of the chambers of the House of Representatives in Washington, D.C. At one point, displeased with the music, he ordered the Marine Band to be present in the service on Sundays and to provide music for the singing of psalms and hymns. The Band was paid out of the federal treasury. No one protested because no one of that generation thought of removing God from the public life of the nation.

As president, Jefferson negotiated a federal treaty with the Kaskaskia Indians, a treaty that, among other things, stipulated that federal funds be made available to pay for Christian missionaries to work with the Indians and for the building of a Christian church in which the Indians could worship.[178]

It should also be noted that the so-called *Jefferson Bible* was not an effort—as the name suggests—on Jefferson's part to produce his own Bible. He never called it a "Bible," and there is no question that it was a project motivated by his high regard for the teachings of Jesus, of which he said, "Of all the systems of morality that have come under my observations, none appear to me so pure as that of Jesus."[179] It represented an effort on Jefferson's part to bring together the ethical teachings of Jesus into a single volume, especially for evangelizing and instructing the American Indians. His high regard for Jesus Christ is also shown by the fact that he closed presidential documents with the appellation, "In the year of our Lord Christ."

As founder of the University of Virginia, Jefferson invited the churches of all sects and denominations to establish schools of instruction adjacent to or within the precincts of the university. He wrote,

> The students of the University will be free and expected to attend religious worship at the establishment of their respective sects, in the morning, and in time to meet their school at the University at its stated hour.[180]

The Truth about "The Wall of Separation"

Jefferson, of course, is the one who used the phrase "wall of separation," not in the Constitution, but in a letter to a group of Baptists. The letter was to assure them that the First Amendment provided a "wall of separation" that would protect them from government intrusion. Modern secularists have turned Jefferson's expression on its head by reinterpreting it to mean a "wall of separation" to keep expressions of faith out of the government. This is a blatant distortion of Jefferson's words and intention.

It was in a letter, dated Jan. 1, 1802, to the Danbury Baptist Association of Connecticut that President Jefferson referred to a "wall of separation" between the church and state. The Baptists were concerned about their status in the new nation and how they would be treated. They had reason for concern, for throughout Europe the Baptists had been an outlawed religious sect, severely persecuted by the state and the state-sanctioned churches, both Catholic and Protestant.

They had also suffered persecution in Colonial America, particularly in Virginia, at the hands of the Anglican Church which had been designated as the official, established church in Virginia. These Baptists wrote to Jefferson because they saw in him an ally and friend who, as Governor of Virginia, had come to their aid when they were marginalized and persecuted by the state of Virginia and its "official" church.

In response, Jefferson quoted that part of the First Amendment that reads, "Congress shall make no law respecting an establishment of religion, or prohibiting the free exercise thereof," and he assured this Baptist association that this meant that, in America, there would be "a wall of separation" that would protect them and any other religious group from the intrusion of the state.

Jefferson quite obviously saw the First Amendment as a unidirectional wall, put in place to keep the government out of the church, not to keep God out of the government. His thinking in this regard reflects the Creator-Redeemer distinction of the Reformation that allowed the state no jurisdiction in matters of faith.

Jefferson's own actions, already noted, demonstrate that he did not see the First Amendment as blocking expressions of faith in public affairs, or even requiring the government to remain neutral in matters of faith. Indeed, this was confirmed by Joseph Story (1779-1845) who served as a Supreme Court justice for thirty-four years from 1811-1845. Commenting on the First Amendment, Story said,

> We are not to attribute this prohibition of a national religious establishment to an indifference in religion, and especially to Christianity, which none could hold in more reverence than the framers of the Constitution.[181]

Was Jefferson attempting to exclude Christian influence from the public and political arenas with his "wall of separation"? Absolutely not! Like Washington, Adams, Franklin and others, Jefferson did not want an official state church—as was the case in Europe—monitoring the religious beliefs and activities of its citizenry.

John Witherspoon (1723-1794)

John Knox Witherspoon was the only ordained minister to sign the Declaration of Independence. As a delegate from New Jersey to the Continental Congress, he was one of its most outspoken and influential members, serving on over one hundred committees. He was involved in drafting the Articles of Confederation, and it was he who authored the calls to prayer and fasting that were published by the Congress during the Revolutionary War.

Witherspoon, who was Scottish, had been a well-known preacher and reformer within the Presbyterian Church in Scotland. He held degrees from the University of St. Andrews and the University of Edinburgh, and he was acclaimed for his vast learning. Totally committed to a

Christian world-view, he once proclaimed, "Cursed is all education that is contrary to Christ." [182] In 1768, he emigrated with his family from Scotland to become president of The College of New Jersey.

In Scotland, Witherspoon had been a "dissenting Protestant," where he had advocated for reform of both the church and civil government according to the Scriptures. His efforts provoked reaction from the authorities and he spent time in prison for his faith. He, therefore, knew by experience the importance of freedom of conscience and religious liberty. He knew that true Christianity was the only source of genuine freedom, and he expressed this in this passage:

> God, grant that in America true religion and civil liberty may be inseparable, and that unjust attempts to destroy the one, may in the issue tend to the support and establishment of both. [183]

Having experienced oppression from the British Crown in Scotland, Witherspoon was appalled to see King George III becoming more and more intrusive in the affairs of the colonies. He was especially concerned by reports that Anglican bishops would be sent to America. Consequently, in 1774, he joined the Committees of Correspondence, and in 1776, he became a member of the Continental Congress.

In his 1776 sermon entitled "The Dominion of Providence Over the Passions of Men," Witherspoon presented a Biblical justification for war with Britain, as well as a reason to expect victory. This sermon was published and widely distributed. It may have been influential in the prominent use of the word "Providence" in the Declaration of Independence.

Witherspoon's influence in America's founding was immense. As president and lecturer at the College of New Jersey, he personally taught and mentored many of the country's earliest leaders. From among his students came thirty-seven judges—three of whom served on the Supreme Court—, twelve members of the Continental Congress, twenty-eight senators and forty-nine congressmen. He personally mentored James Madison, the fourth President and chief architect of the U.S. Constitution. Novak calls Witherspoon, "The most influential academic in American history."[184]

Would Witherspoon have gone along with a secular government that excluded Christianity from the public square. Absolutely not!

Charles Carroll (1737-1832)

Charles Carrol was the only Roman Catholic Founding Father. A wealthy landowner, he outlived every other signer of the Declaration of Independence. Although initially not interested in politics, Carroll became a vocal critic of King George and the British attempts to tax and regulate the lives of the American colonists. His bold advocacy for independence brought him to the attention of other patriots, and he soon found himself being embraced by others of like thinking. He became a delegate to the Continental Congress and was a signer of the Declaration of Independence. He later served as a senator from Maryland.

Carrol expressed a deep faith in Jesus Christ, which may show an influence from the Great Awakening where faith in Christ, rather than religious ritual and church affiliation, was emphasized. For example, in a letter to a friend, he declared, "On the mercy of my Redeemer I rely for salvation and on His merits; not on the works I have done in obedience to His precepts."[185]

In 1826, as the last surviving signer of the Declaration of Independence, the City of New York requested from Carroll a copy of the document for deposit in the public hall. He complied with their request and appended the following comment to the document.

> Grateful to Almighty God for the blessings which, through Jesus Christ our Lord, He has conferred on my beloved country in her emancipation and on myself in permitting me, under circumstances of mercy, to live to the age of eighty-nine years, and to survive the fiftieth year of American independence. I do hereby recommend to the present and future generations the principles of that important document as the best inheritance their ancestors could bequeath to them, and pray that the civil and religious liberties they have secured to my country may be perpetuated to remotest posterity and extended to the whole family of man.[186]

The Catholic Embrace of America

Although America was obviously founded on the philosophical and theological presuppositions of the Radical Reformation, Roman Catholics soon came to see the value of the unique American political experiment. This has been laid out by the Catholic scholar, William Novak, in his excellent book entitled *On Two Wings: Humble Faith and Common Sense at the American Founding*.

He cites, for example, how Cardinal Gibbons of Baltimore expressed his admiration for America in Rome in 1887 at the time of his installation as a Cardinal. Gibbons said,

> For myself, as a citizen of the United States, and without closing my eyes to our shortcomings as a nation, I say with a deep sense of pride and gratitude that I belong to a country where the civil government holds over us the aegis of its protection, without interfering with us in the legitimate exercise of our sublime mission as ministers of the Gospel of Christ. Our country has liberty without license, and authority with despotism.[187]

Novak also quotes Pope John Paul II, who expressed commendable understanding of America's founding and of the responsibility of each generation to understand and embrace the nation's founding principles. John Paul wrote,

> The continuing success of American democracy depends on the degree to which each new generation, native-born and immigrant, makes its own the moral truths on which the Founding Fathers staked the future of your Republic."[188]

The Founders and Slavery

If a foreign visitor had read the Constitution at the time

of its enactment, they would not have known that slavery existed in America. There is no mention of slaves or slavery. There is no reference to individuals on the basis of race, ethnicity, or skin color. Instead of using race classifications, the Constitution speak of "citizens," "persons," and "other persons."

There is nothing in the Declaration of Independence and the United States Constitution to indicate that the freedoms guaranteed do not apply to every individual. Dr. Martin Luther King, Jr. understood this, and in his stirring "I Have a Dream" speech, he challenged America, not to dispense with its founding documents, but instead, to live up to them. He declared his hope

> ... that one day this nation will rise up and live out the true meaning of its creed: "We hold these truths to be self-evident, that all men are created equal."

Showing that he understood these freedoms to be rooted in the country's Christian origins, Dr. King, who was a devout Christian, went on to say that he had a dream that one day all Americans—whether white or black—would be able to sing together the words of that Christian, patriotic hymn,

> *My country 'tis of Thee,*
> *Sweet land of liberty, of Thee I sing.*
> *Land where my fathers died,*
> *Land of the Pilgrim's pride,*
> *From every mountainside,*
> *Let freedom ring!*

America's founding principles are colorblind, even if her

history has not been. The famous abolitionist, Frederick Douglas, understood this and argued that the language of the founding documents must be understood as applying to everyone. "Anyone of these provisions in the hands of abolition statesmen, and backed by a right moral sentiment," he declared, "would put an end to slavery in America."

One of the most misunderstood sections of the Constitution is the "three-fifths clause" in which only three-fifths of the slave population of southern states would be counted for representation. This had nothing to do with assigning value based on race. This was related to keeping the southern states from gaining too much power in the new Congress where the number of representatives from each state would be tied to the population of that state.

The southern states wanted to include their slave populations to gain more representatives and more power, even though slaves could not vote. The three-fifths compromise was a way of diminishing their influence in the new Congress in that it counted only three-fifths of the slave population for purposes of representation.

Even here, the Founders did not use the word "slaves" or slavery," but "other persons." Abraham Lincoln described this refusal of the Founders to acknowledge slavery in the Constitution as being like a man who hides an ugly, cancerous growth until the time comes that it can be eradicated from his body.

That the three-fifths clause had nothing to do with assigning value based on race is confirmed by the fact that, at the time of the Constitutional Convention, there were at least sixty-thousand free blacks in northern and southern states who counted the same as whites when it came to determining the number of representatives to Congress. Additionally, it is important to note that there were as many as ten states where blacks had full voting privileges.

At the Constitutional Convention, concessions were made toward the southern states because of concern that a union could not succeed if all Thirteen Colonies were not included. The Founders, however, were both careful and precise in the use of language. They referred to slaves as "persons" and never used the words "black" or "white," "slave" or "slavery." Though not banning slavery outright at the time, they put in place the legal mines that would eventually blow up the institution of slavery.

George Mason of Virginia, however, argued against such concessions and pushed for the immediate outlawing of slavery. He warned of the judgment of God, if slavery were allowed to continue, saying,

> Every master is born a petty tyrant. They bring the judgment of Heaven upon a country. As nations cannot be rewarded or punished in the next world, they must be in this. By an inevitable chain of causes and effects, Providence punishes national sins by national calamities.[189]

Many see the Civil War, with the loss of 700,000 lives, as the judgment predicted by Mason. Thomas Jefferson shared Mason's concern, for it was in the context of the continued existence of slavery that he wrote,

> God who gave us life, gave us liberty. And can the

liberties of a nation be thought secure when we have removed their only firm basis, a conviction in the minds of the people that these liberties are a gift from God? That they are not to be violated but with His wrath? Indeed, I tremble for my country when I reflect that God is just and that His justice cannot sleep forever.[190]

With this sort of Biblical and moral opposition to slavery at the nation's founding, it is easy to see how its days were already numbered. Most of the Founders who happened to be slave owners set their slaves free. Two years before the Constitutional Convention, Benjamin Franklin set his two slaves free and began to advocate for abolition. George Washington's situation was more complex, for he had inherited a large plantation with a number of slaves and to thrust them suddenly and unprepared out into the world would have been unwise, perhaps harmful to them.

Washington, therefore, set in motion a compassionate program to disentangle Mt. Vernon completely from the institution of slavery. Those slaves who wanted to leave were free to do so. Those who chose to remain were paid wages, and he began a program to educate and prepare the children of slaves for freedom. He declared,

I clearly foresee that nothing but the rooting out of slavery can perpetuate the existence of our union by consolidating it in a common bond of principle.[191]

Secularists love to insist that America was founded on racist principles. They are wrong. David Azerrad was correct when he said, "The argument that the Constitution is racist suffers from one fatal flaw: the concept of race does not exist in the Constitution."[192]

The Founders did not invent slavery. They were born into a world where slavery already existed. They were not perfect, and it can be argued that they conceded too much at the time. Nonetheless, they did an admirable job of formulating founding documents that would eventually eradicate that horrendous institution and make America "the land of the free and home of the brave," with people of every race and ethnicity wanting to live here.

One Nation Under God

> Our laws and our institutions must necessarily
> be based upon and embody the teachings of
> The Redeemer of mankind.
> It is impossible that it should be otherwise;
> and in this sense and to this extent our civilization
> and our institutions are emphatically Christian.
>
> The U.S. Supreme Court, 1892

Expressions such as "One Nation Under God," which is found in the Pledge of Allegiance, "In God We Trust," found on all U.S. currency, and "God Bless America"—a common expression of presidents and politicians—are all remnants from the founding generation when faith in God was part of being American.

The Christian mindset of the Founders was affirmed in a ten-year project to discover where they got their ideas for America's founding documents. The study found that by far the single most cited authority in their writings was the Bible.[193] It comes then as no surprise that John Adams, nearly four decades after the American Revolution, would declare,

The general principles on which the fathers achieved independence were . . . the general principles of Christianity. Now I will avow that I then believed, and now believe, that those general principles of Christianity are as eternal and immutable as the existence and attributes of God.[194]

In spite of overwhelming evidence to the contrary, secularists love to argue that the Founders were profoundly influenced by the Enlightenment, simply because they sometimes quote Enlightenment and pagan philosophers. This, however, merely shows that they had an excellent liberal education in classical history and philosophy. The people of Colonial America were probably the best educated in the world at the time of the American Revolution.

The Influence of John Locke

The Founders were especially fond of the British philosopher, John Locke (1632-1704), who is widely regarded as one of the most influential of Enlightenment thinkers. Secularists have seized upon this as evidence of the influence of the Enlightenment on the Founders. Such an interpretation, however, reveals a lack of understanding of the facts.

Locke was thoroughly Christian in his thinking. Born of Puritan stock, his social and political theories, such as the social-compact theory and the idea that "those who govern must do so only with the consent of the governed" were more a product of the Separatist Puritan tradition than of the Enlightenment. He emphasized reason, but believed that honest reasoning would lead to a belief in the existence of the God of the Bible.

In his book, *The Reasonableness of Christianity*, Locke utilizes both reason and the revelation of Scripture to make his case for the veracity of Christianity. Arguing from Scripture and miracles, he writes,

> The evidence of Our Savior's mission from heaven is so great, in the multitude of miracles He did, before all sorts of people, that what He delivered cannot but be received as the oracles of God. For the miracles He did were so ordered by the divine providence and wisdom, that they never were, nor could be denied by any of the enemies or opposers of Christianity.[195]

Concerning reason, Locke insisted that the pagan world remained in darkness because they made so little use of their reason. Instead of using their rational faculties, which would lead them to the one true God, they allowed themselves to be bound by animal passions such as lust, fear, and carelessness, which then made them vulnerable to false religions. "It was in this state of darkness and error," said Locke, "that our Savior found the world."[196]

Locke's influence, therefore, was not away from Christianity. Instead, his influence on the Founders was toward Christianity, and a political system, based on both revelation and reason.

The Testimony of a Chief Justice

That America was founded on Christian ideals that

emerged from the Reformation is obvious, not only from the testimonies of the Founders themselves, but also from the testimonies of those who were closest to them in time and space.

A good example of such a person is John Marshall (1755-1835), who served as the second Chief Justice of the U.S. Supreme Court for thirty-four years (1801-1835). Many consider him the greatest Chief Justice the court has known. During his tenure, he heard many cases and offered groundbreaking opinions that continue to guide the Supreme Court and the United States Government today.

In one of his writings, Marshall clearly states what every Founder assumed that the founding documents and institutions on which the nation was formed presuppose a commitment to Christian principles and values. He wrote,

> No person, I believe, questions the importance of religion in the happiness of man, even during his existence in this world. The American population is entirely Christian, and with us Christianity and religion are identified. It would be strange, indeed, if with such a people, our institutions did not presuppose Christianity, and did not refer to it, and exhibit relations with it.[197]

While Chief Justice, Marshall made the Supreme Court facilities available to a local congregation for their Sunday gatherings. So each Sunday, the singing of Christian hymns and the preaching of God's Word could be heard ringing through the chambers of both the House of Representatives and the Supreme Court. This was neither surprising nor offensive to anyone, for it fit perfectly within the mindset of the founding generation.

The merger of faith and freedom was still a part of the American mindset as recent as 1892, when in the ruling of Church of the Holy Trinity *vs* The United States, the United States Supreme Court declared,

> Our laws and our institutions must necessarily be based upon and embody the teachings of The Redeemer of mankind. It is impossible that it should be otherwise; and in this sense and to this extent our civilization and our institutions are emphatically Christian ... From the discovery of this continent to the present hour, there is a single voice making this affirmation ... we find everywhere a clear recognition of the same truth that this is a Christian nation.

This clear statement, made by the nation's highest Court after investigating thousands of historical documents, has been rejected by modern culture. From the Whitehouse to the Schoolhouse, we are told that America is not a Christian nation, but was founded by Deists and secularists on secular, Enlightenment thinking. This falsehood must be reversed if the America of Washington, Jefferson and our parents is to survive.

A French Sociologist Gets the Picture

That America's founders did not separate God from government was obvious to the young French sociologist, Alexis de Tocqueville, who came to America in 1831 to study her institutions. He wanted to see if he could discover the reason for America's rapid rise to power and affluence in the world.

Arriving on the heels of the Second Great Awakening, he exclaimed, "The religious atmosphere of the country was the first thing that struck me on arrival in the United States." He also observed that the means of improving the government were the same means employed in conversion and the advancement of the Christian faith. He concluded that, in America, "From the beginning, politics and religion contracted an alliance which has never been dissolved."[198]

Different Gods & Different Revolutions

Tocqueville also noted the obvious difference between the American Revolution and the French Revolution, in which there was a rejection, not only of a national church, but also of the God of the Bible. Being predominately Roman Catholic, the French did not have a sense of distinction between God and church as did the English dissenting Protestants, who rejected the state churches, but clung to their faith in God. The French revolutionists rejected, not only church, but also God, replacing the God of the Bible with the god (or goddess) of human reason.

The French "Declaration of the Rights of Man," therefore, did not acknowledge human rights as having their source in the Creator, as did the American Declaration, nor did it state that rights are inherent. With no higher moral guide than human reason and experience, the French Revolution soon descended into anarchy with twenty thousand people being executed because they were considered enemies of the new regime. Hart says,

> The French Revolution is a grim example of how people behave when they are unchecked by a sense of religious obligation.[199]

It is no wonder that George Washington warned America to maintain "religion"[200] [i.e., Christianity] and morality in order to preserve political and social stability.

Washington's Farewell Warning

In his Farewell Address after serving two terms as America's first President, George Washington warned the young nation to guard against the very trends that are being embraced and promoted in America today. He said,

> Of all the dispositions and habits which lead to political prosperity, religion and morality are *indispensable* supports. In vain would that man claim the tribute of patriotism, who should labor to subvert these great pillars of human happiness, these firmest props of the duties of men and citizens. The mere politician, equally with the pious man, ought to respect and to cherish them. And let us with caution indulge the supposition that morality can be maintained without religion. Whatever may be conceded to the influence of refined education on minds of peculiar structure, reason and experience both forbid us to expect that

national morality can prevail in exclusion of religious principle.

Washington says that religion [i.e., Christianity] and morality are indispensable supports for political prosperity, and he warns against the supposition that morality could be sustained without Christianity. In other words, he warns against any attempt to separate God from the state; that is, against trying to secularize the American political system. This is why Mark Hall, Professor of Politics at George Fox University, says,

America's Founders did not want Congress to establish a national church, and many opposed establishments at the state level, as well. Yet they believed, as George Washington declared in his Farewell Address, that of "all the dispositions and habits which lead to political prosperity, religion and morality are indispensable supports." Moreover, almost without exception, they agreed that civic authorities could promote and encourage Christianity and that it was appropriate for elected officials to make religious arguments in the public square. There was virtually no support for contemporary visions of a separation of church and state that would have political leaders avoid religious language and require public spaces to be stripped of religious symbols.[201]

Who Represents the Founders Today?

Washington and all of the Founders would be shocked at President Barack Obama ordering the removal of a

Christian symbol from behind the podium when he spoke at Georgetown University, a Roman Catholic institution. They would be appalled at the lawsuits that are filed on a regular basis seeking to remove Christian symbols and expressions of prayer and faith from the public life of the nation.

Such attempts to secularize America and remove every vestige of Christianity from its public life are completely out of character with this nation's origins. It is, in fact, the committed follower of Christ who loves America who has the most in common with America's Founders. It is the individual who, in the words of the Pledge of Allegiance, has a vision for "one nation under God" that is closest to the founding generation.

Will America Survive?

> Our Constitution was made only for a moral and
> religious people. It is wholly inadequate
> to the government of any other.
>
> *John Adams, Second President of the U.S.A.*

At the closing banquet celebrating the Constitutional Convention, a Philadelphia matron rushed toward its most senior member, Benjamin Franklin, and gushed, "O Mister Franklin, what have you gentlemen wrought?" Franklin is said to have paused, adjusted his glasses and solemnly replied, "A republic madam. If you can keep it."

Franklin was solemn because in a "republic," freedoms are guaranteed to the people by a Constitution and Bill of Rights. Franklin knew that those same freedoms they had just enshrined could be turned into anarchy by a populace that did not have the capacity to govern itself according to internal moral principles.

He and all the Founders knew that the success of the nation they had formed hinged on the moral character of its citizens and their ability to govern themselves according to Biblical principles. This is why John Adams, in a 1798 address to the officers of the Massachusetts Militia, declared,

> We have no government armed with power capable of contending with human passions unbridled by morality and religion . . . Our Constitution was made only for a moral and religious people. It is wholly inadequate to the government of any other."[202]

James Madison also recognized that the freedoms they had instituted hinged on the American populace governing themselves according to Judeo/Christian principles. This is the context of his statement:

> We have staked the whole future of the American civilization, not upon the power of government, far from it. We have staked the future . . . upon the capacity of each and all of us to govern ourselves according to the Ten Commandments.[203]

Faith & Freedom Go Hand-in-Hand

This recognition of the vital role of Christianity for the success of the Republic was pervasive in the founding generation. Two weeks before the adoption of the Declaration of Independence, John Adams wrote to his cousin, Zabdiel, a minister of the Gospel, and exhorted him in this regard:

> Statesmen, my dear sir, may plan and speculate for Liberty, but it is Religion and Morality alone, which can establish the Principles, upon which Freedom can securely stand.[204]

We may recall the words of George Washington in his Farewell Address that the *indispensable* supports of political prosperity are "religion and morality." When the Founders use the word "religion," they are referring to Christianity. For Washington, Christianity was not something to be tolerated in the new nation; rather, it was something *indispensable* for the nation's survival and success. Washington elaborated on this when he wrote,

> The propitious smiles of Heaven can never be expected on a nation that disregards the external rules of order and right, which Heaven itself has ordained."[205]

The Founders were unanimous in their belief that only a virtuous and moral people could maintain the liberties enshrined in the founding documents. They were also unanimous in the belief that such morality and virtue could only be derived from a revived and vibrant Christianity. As Novak says,

> Far from having a hostility toward religion, the founders counted on religion [Christianity] for the underlying philosophy of the republic, its supporting ethic, and its reliable source of rejuvenation.[206]

The Unique Challenge Today

Today, however, the America of Washington, Jefferson, Lincoln, our parents, and grandparents, is rapidly fading into oblivion. While the modern church has been enamored with finding acceptance and approval in modern society, historical revisionists have been quietly

174

at work severing the nation from its Christian roots. For the secularist, this is a major achievement, for to fundamentally transform a nation, its history must first be transformed. This is what Alexander Solzhenitsyn was referring to when he said, "To destroy a people, you must first sever their roots."[207]

Severed from its Christian past, America seems defenseless against the moral relativism and subjective, political-correctness that is permeating the culture. With the loss of its Christian heritage, America's populace is now vulnerable, in a way it has never been, to being shaped into an amoral, secularist society. American culture has now reached the point, spoken of by Karl Marx when he said, "A people without a heritage are easily persuaded."

Recovering Our Heritage

America must regain its true heritage if it is to survive, and in this regard, we can take a lesson from the Jewish people. The Hebrews have survived because no enemy has been able to sever them from their historical roots. No enemy has been able to re-write their history. Through wars, dispersions, pogroms, and holocausts, they have maintained their identity as the descendants of Abraham, Isaac, Jacob, and Moses. Even in times of distress, each generation has been diligent to teach its children their true heritage, not only in words, but through the festivals that are faithfully observed every year. The importance of maintaining their history was highlighted by the Psalmist who wrote,

For He established a testimony in Jacob and appointed a law in Israel, which He commanded our fathers, that they should make them known to their children; that the generation to come might know them, the children who would be born, that they may arise and declare them to their children, that they may set their hope in God . . . (Psalm 78:1-7).

If the America of Washington, Franklin, Jefferson, and Lincoln is to survive, Christians must take the lead in teaching their children the true story of America. We must highlight the faith of the Pilgrims and Patriots who were willing to forsake all for their vision of a nation where faith and freedom would dwell together without molestation and conflict. We must recount the stories of Edwards, Whitefield, and Brainerd. We must tell and retell the story of the Great Awakening and the role it played in giving birth to America. We must take back our history.

Spiritual Awakening
A "Must" for This Generation

Because the God of history is also the God of "the now," we must also pray for another great, Spiritual awakening in our land. We must not look to Washington, D.C., for the solution to America's ills. The answer for America will not begin at the White House, but at God's House.

I Peter 4:17 says, *For the time has come for judgment to begin at the house of God.* This means that we, as Christians and Christian leaders, must lead the way in evaluating our lives in light of the teachings of Jesus and the New Testament, and offering repentance and confession where necessary. As the church acknowledges its "backsliding" and compromise with the world, God will answer with *times of refreshing from the presence of the Lord,* as promised in Acts 3:19.

This describes the experience of one particular church during the Second Great Awakening, as described by Charles Finney. The leaders of this church came to realize that in seeking acceptance and recognition from the culture, they had compromised their commitment to Christ. They, therefore, formulated a public statement concerning their "backsliding and want of a Christian spirit."[208] It was submitted to the congregation for their approval and then read before the congregation. As the confession was being read publicly, the entire congregation stood to its feet with many of its members weeping. Finney said that, from that moment on, the revival went forward in power, and the opposition, which had been bitter, was silenced.

How American Can Be Great Again

This critical role of an awakened Christianity in the life of America is affirmed in a quote from an unknown visitor to this country, probably in the first half of the nineteenth century. This visitor, who was obviously searching for the secret to America's rapid rise to affluence and power, recounts how he sought for the secret of America's greatness in her form of government, her educational system, her vast commerce, and so on.

Instead, he found it in something else—something astounding:

> Not until I went into the churches of America and heard her pulpits flame with righteousness did I understand the secret of her genius and power. America is great because America is good, and if America ever ceases to be good, America will cease to be great.[209]

America can be great again, not by seeking greatness, but by seeking God. America can be great again, not by running from her past, but by reconnecting with her past and learning from her Founders, who like the searching visitor, tied America's future greatness to her ability to maintain her goodness.

As we reconnect with our radical Christian roots and ask God to visit this nation once again with Spiritual Awakening, America's current course will be altered. A national healing will occur, not instigated by a new program from Washington, D.C., but sent down from Heaven as promised in II Chronicles 7:14. When that happens, all Americans will be able to sing, with thankfulness of heart, that patriotic hymn that says,

America! America!
God shed His grace on Thee.
And crown Thy good,
With brotherhood,
From sea to shining sea.

Selected Bibliography

Amos, Gary and Richard Gardiner. *Never Before in History: America's Inspired Birth*. Richardson, TX: Foundation for Thought and Ethics, 1998.

Barton, David. *The Role of Pastors & Christians in Civil Government*. Aledo, TX: WallBuilder Press, 2003.

Bradford, William. *Of Plymouth Plantation 1620-1647*. Samuel Eliot Morison, Ed. New York: Alfred A. Knoff, 2011.

Edwards, Jonathan. *Jonathan Edwards on Revival*. Carlisle, PA: Banner of Truth Trust, 1994.

Franklin, Benjamin. *The Autobiography of Benjamin Franklin*. New York: Airmont, 1965.

Hall, Verna M., Ed. *The Christian History of the American Revolution*. San Francisco: The Foundation for Christian Education, 1976.

Hart, Benjamin. *Faith & Freedom: The Christian Roots of American Liberty*. Dallas: Lewis and Stanley, 1988.

Hyatt, Eddie L. *The Faith & Vision of Benjamin Franklin*. Grapevine, TX: Hyatt Press, 2015.

Kennedy, D. James and Jerry Newcombe. *What If America Were a Christian Nation Again?* Nashville: Thomas Nelson, 2003.

Marshall, Peter and David Manuel. *The Light and the Glory*. Grand Rapids: Fleming H. Revell, 1977.

Mourt's Relation: A Journal of Pilgrims at Plymouth. Dwight B. Heath, Ed. Bedford, MA: Applewood Books, 1622. *reprint* 1963.

Novak, William. *On Two Wings: Humble Faith and Common Sense at the American Founding*. San Francisco: Encounter Books, 2002.

Whitefield, George. *George Whitefield's Journals*. Carlisle, PA: Banner of Truth Trust, 1960.

End Notes

[1] This quote is found in numerous online sources.

[2] Michael Novak, Two Wings: *Humble Faith and Common Sense at the American Founding* (San Francisco: Encounter Books, 2002), 5.

[3] Novak, 5.

[4] George H. Williams, *Radical Reformation* (Louisville: Westminster John Knox Press, 1962).

[5] William Bradford, *Of Plymouth Plantation 1620-1647*, ed. Samuel Eliot Morrison (New York: Alfred A. Knopf, 2011), 431.

[6] Benjamin Franklin, *The Autobiography of Benjamin Franklin* (New York: Airmont, 1965), 100.

[7] William Bradford, *Of Plymouth Plantation 1620-1647*, ed. Samuel Eliot Morrison (New York: Alfred A. Knopf, 2011), 9

[8] Philip Schaff, vol. 7 of *History of the Christian Church* (Grand Rapids: Eerdmans, 1910, 304-05.

[9] Schaff, 304-05

[10] Bradford, 8.

[11] Bradford, 9.

[12] Peter Marshall and David Manuel, *The Light and the Glory* (Grand Rapids: Fleming H. Revell, 1977), 108.

[13] Bradford, xxxiii.

[14] Bradford, 9.

[15] Bradford, 12-15.

[16] William Bradford, *Of Plymouth Plantation 1620-1647*, ed. Samuel Eliot Morrison (New York: Alfred A. Knopf, 2011), 19.

[17] Bradford, 18.

[18] Benjamin Hart, *Faith & Freedom* (Dallas: Lewis and Stanley, 1988), 71.

[19] Bradford, 25.

[20] Bradford, 47.

[21] Bradford, 48.

[22] Bradford, 47.

[23] Bradford, 61.

[24] Bradford, 89.

[25] Dwight B. Heath, ed., *Mourt's Relation: A Journal of the Pilgrims of New England* (Bedford, MA: Applewood Books, 1963), 79.

[26] *Mourt's Relation*, 79.

[27] *Mourt's Relation*, 82-83

[28] *Mourt's Relation*, 82

[29] *Mourt's Relation*, 82

[30] Bradford, 131

[31] Bradford, 131-32.

[32] Bradford, 120-21.

[33] Benjamin Hart, *Faith & Freedom* (Dallas: Lewis and Stanley, 1988), 82.

[34] Hart, 87.

[35] Hart, 88

[36] Hart, 88.

[37] Hart, 93.

[38] Perry Miller, *An Errand into the Wilderness* (Cambridge, MA: The President and Fellows of Harvard College, 1984), 11.

[39] Henry Martyn Dexter, "The Congregationalism of the Last Three Hundred Years," Verna M. Hall, ed., *The Christian History of the American Revolution* (San Francisco: Foundation for American Christian Education, 1975), 89.

[40] Dexter, "The Congregationalism of the Last Three Hundred Years," 90.

[41] Hart, 94

[42] John Thornton Wingate, "The Pulpit of the American Revolution," Verna M. Hall, ed., *The Christian History of the American Revolution* (San Francisco: The Foundation for American Christian Education, 1973), 191.

[43] Mark A. Noll, *A History of Christianity in the United States and Canada* (Grand Rapids: Eerdmans, 1996), 47.

[44] Gary Amos and Richard Gardiner, *Never Before in History: America's Inspired Birth* (Dallas: Haughton, 1998), 44.

[45] Gary Amos and Richard Gardiner, 43.

[46] Hart, 77.

[47] Gary Amos and Richard Gardiner, 76.

[48] Earle E. Cairns, *Christianity through the Centuries* (Grand Rapids: Zondervan, 1981), 366.

[49] Noll, 44.

[50] Noll, 40.

[51] Bradford, 431.

[52] Bradford, 431

[53] Bradford, 434.

[54] Bradford, 434.

[55] Peter Marshall and David Manuel, *The Light and the Glory* (Grand Rapids: Fleming H. Revell, 1977), 72.

[56] Noll, 37.

[57] Hart, 151.

[58] George H. Williams, *Spiritual and Anabaptist Writers*, vol. 2 of *The Library of Christian Classics* (London: SCM Press, 1957), 25.

[59] Bradford, 257.

[60] Rufus M. Jones, ed., *George Fox: An Autobiography* (Philadelphia: Ferris and Leach, 1919), 82.

[61] Hart, 205.

[62] http://www.straight-talk.net/socas/s-summary.shtml.

[63] Hart, 64.

[64] Marshall Foster and Mary-Elaine Swanson, *The American Covenant, The Untold Story* (USA: The Mayflower Institute, 1983), 158-59.

[65] Bradford wrote, "O sacred bond, whilst inviolaby preserved. How sweet and precious were the fruits that flowed from the same! But when this fidelity decayed, then their ruin approached. O that these ancient members had not died or been dissipated (if it had been the will of God) or else that this holy care and constant faithfulness had still lived, and remained with those that survived," 33.

[66] Bradford, xxvii.

[67] Peter Marshall and David Manuel, 216.

[68] Peter Marshall and David Manuel, 237.

[69] Noll, 51.

[70] Peter Marshall and David Manuel, 238-39.

[71] Jonathan Edwards, *Jonathan Edwards on Revival* (Carlisle, PA: Banner of Truth Trust, 1994), 77.

[72] Edwards, 77.

[73] Jonathan Edwards, 77.

[74] George Whitefield, *George Whitefield's Journals* (Carlisle, PA: The Banner of Truth Trust, 1960), 352.

[75] Earle E. Cairns, 366.

[76] David O. Beale, "The Log College," *Faith of Our Fathers: Scenes from American Church History*, Mark Sidwell, ed. (Greenville, SC: BJU Press, 1991), 40-43.

[77] George Whitefield, *George Whitefield's Journals* (Carlisle, PA: Banner of Truth Trust, 1960), 347.

[78] David O. Beale, "The Log College," 40-43.

[79] Charles Hodge, "The Constitutional History of the Presbyterian Church in the United States," Verna M. Hall, ed., *The Christian History of the American Revolution* (San Francisco: The Foundation for Christian Education, 1976), 123.

[80] David S. Lovejoy, *Religious Enthusiasm and the Great Awakening* (Englewood Cliffs, NJ: Prentice Hall, 1969), 5.

[81] Whitefield, 477.

[82] Edwards, 13.

[83] Edwards, 13.

[84] Edwards, 24.

[85] Edwards, 24.

[86] Edwards, 19.

[87] Edwards, 14.

[88] Edwards, 15.

[89] Edwards, 16.

[90] William Sweet, *Revivalism in America* (New York: Abingdon, 1944), 30.

[91] Jonathan Edwards, 3.

[92] Christine Leigh Heyrman, "The First Great Awakening," http://nationalhumanitiescenter.org/tserve/eighteen/ekeyinfo/gra waken.htm

[93] Sarah Pierpont Edwards, http://xroads.virginia.edu/~ma05/peltier/conversion/pierpont2.html.

[94] Seno Dwight, vol. 1 of *The Works of President Edwards: With a Memoir of His life* (New York: G & C & C Carvill, 1836), 171-186; http://xroads.virginia.edu/~ma05/peltier/conversion/pierpont2.html

[95] "The Women in Jonathan Edwards' Life," http://cogitavi.wordpress.com/2010/10/06/the-women-in-jonathan-edwards-life/.

[96] For a thorough discussion of this phenomena among women, see Susan Hyatt, *In the Spirit We're Equal* (Dallas: Hyatt Press, 1998).

[97] "Patriotic Women and Home Sentiment," Verna M. Hall, ed., *The Christian History of the American Revolution* (San Francisco: Foundation for American Christian Education, 1975), 73-86; David Barton, "Glen Beck," The Fox News Channel, May 27, 2011.

[98] See Timothy Smith, *Revivalism and Social Reform in Mid-Nineteenth Century America*, who shows that modern civil rights movements have their roots in American revivalism.

[99] Diary of David Brainerd, http://www.eternallifeministries.org/brainerd.htm, April 19, 1742.

[100] Richard A. Hasler, *Journey with David Brainerd* (Downers Grove: InterVarsity Press, 1975), 80-81

[101] Hasler, 92.

[102] Collin G. Calloway, "American Indians and the American Revolution," http://www.nps.gov/revwar/about_the_revolution/american_indians. html.

[103] Mark A. Noll, 106.

[104] Jonathan Edwards, 20.

[105] http://www.chitorch.org/index.php/chm/seventeenth-century/slave-religion/2/

[106] Whitefield, 420.

[107] Whitefield, 420.

[108] Thomas S. Kidd, *George Whitefield:* America's *Spiritual Founding Father* (New Haven: Yale University Press, 2014), 114.

[109] Noll, 106-07.

[110] T. Harry Williams, Richard N. Current, and Frank Freidel, *A History of the United States to 1877* (New York: Random House, 1959), 132.

[111] David Barton, "Glen Beck," The Fox News Channel, May 27, 2011.

[112] Hart, 330.

[113] See Timothy Smith, *Revivalism and Social Reform in Mid-Nineteenth Century America* (New York City: Harper & Rowe, 1965).

[114] George Whitefield, *George Whitefield's Journals* (London: The Banner of Truth Trust, 1965), 310.

[115] http://www.washingtonubf.org/Resources/ Leaders/GeorgeWhitefield.html.

[116] Benjamin Franklin, *The Autobiography of Benjamin Franklin* (New York City: Airmont Publishing, 1965), 100.

[117] Franklin, 103

[118] Peter Marshall and David Manuel, 248.

[119] George Whitefield, *George Whitefield's Journals* (London: The Banner of Truth Trust, 1965), 425.

[120] Thomas S. Kidd, *George Whitefield: America's Spiritual Founding Father* (New Haven: Yale University Press, 2014), 211.

[121] See my book, *The Faith & Vision of Benjamin Franklin* (Grapevine, TX: Hyatt Press, 2015).

[122] Kidd, 251

[123] Kidd, 253.

[124] See Kidd, *George Whitefield: America's Spiritual Founding Father.*

[125] Eddie Hyatt, *2000 Years of Charismatic Christianity* (Lake Mary, FL: Charisma House, 2002), 112.

[126] "Christian History of the Ivy League Universities," http://jeremybardwell.wordpress.com/2010/03/26/christian-history-of-the-ivy-league-universities/.

[127] Hart, 224.

[128] T. Harry Williams, Richard N. Current, and Frank Freidel, *A History of the United States to 1877* (New York: Random House, 1959), 132.

[129] David Ramsey, "Prelude to the American Revolution, 1765-1775," Verna M. Hall, ed., *The Christian History of the American Revolution* (San Francisco: The Foundation for American Christian Education, 1975), 435.

[130] Hart, 238.

[131] Hart, 260.

[132] Hart, 239.

[133] Novak, 17.

[134] Hart, 271.

[135] These figures are from Ramsay, "Prelude to the American Revolution, 1765-1775," 492.

[136] Peter Marshall and David Manuel, 267. See also Amos and Gardiner, 124.

[137] Peter Marshall and David Manuel, 267.

[138] Michael Novak, *On Two Wings: Humble Faith and Common Sense at the American Founding* (San Francisco: Encounter, 2002), 14.

[139] Novak, 18.

[140] Novak, 18.

[141] Novak, 22.

[142] Novak, 21.

[143] Hart, 234

[144] Novak, 19.

[145] Hart, 293.

[146] Arnold "Friberg, The Prayer at Valley Forge, " http://www.revolutionary-war-and-beyond.com/prayer-at-valley-forge.html.

[147] Novak, 33.

[148] Novak, 157-58.

[149] Novak, 20.

[150] Amos and Gardiner, 56.

[151] Amos and Gardiner, 56.

[152] Bill Bright and John N. Damoose, "Faith of our Fathers," *Pentecostal Evangel*, no. 4442 (June 27, 1999), 9-11.

[153] Hart, 228.

[154] Charles Hodge, "The Constitutional History of the Presbyterian Church in the United Stated," Verna M. Hall, ed., *The Christian History of the American Revolution* (San Francisco: The Foundation for American Christian Education, 1975), 123

[155] Peter Marshall and David Manuel, 284.

[156] Peter Marshall and David Manuel, 285.

[157] Bill Bright and John Damoose, "Faith of Our Fathers," 9.

[158] David Barton, "James Madison and Religion in Public," http://www.wallbuilders.com/LIBissuesArticles.asp?id=105.

[159] Bill Bright and John Damoose, "Faith of Our Fathers," 9.

[160] Hart, 232.

[161] See Eddie Hyatt, *The Faith & Vision of Benjamin Franklin* (Grapevine, TX: Hyatt Press, 2015), 10-12.

[162] Hyatt, *The Faith & Vision of Benjamin Franklin,* 26.

[163] Franklin, 102.

[164] Eddie Hyatt, *The Faith & Vision of Benjamin Franklin* (Grapevine, TX: Hyatt Press, 2015), 38.

[165] Franklin, 108.

[166] This letter is in the Library of Congress and is referred to by various writers.

[167] Franklin, 79.

[168] Franklin, 79.

[169] Franklin, 42.

[170] Franklin, 159.

[171] Hyatt, *The Faith & Vision of Benjamin Franklin*, 62-63.

[172] David Barton, "James Madison and Religion in Public," http://www.wallbuilders.com/LIBissuesArticles.asp?id=105.

[173] Barton, "James Madison and Religion in Public," http://www.wallbuilders.com/LIBissuesArticles.asp?id=105.

[174] D. James Kennedy with Jerry Newcombe, *What If America Were A Christian Nation Again?* (Nashville: Thomas Nelson, 2003), 89.

[175] From Madison's "Detached Memoranda," http://candst.tripod.com/detach.htm

[176] Novak, 59-60.

[177] David Barton, *Original Intent* (Aledo, TX: WallBuilder Press, 2000), 144.

[178] Barton, *The Role of Pastors & Christians in Civil Government*, 24.

[179] Thomas Jefferson to William Camby, 18 Sept. 1813, *Writings*, XIII: 377; cited in D. James Kennedy, *What if America Were a Christian Nation Again* (Nashville: Thomas Nelson, 2003), 46.

[180] Hart, 351.

[181] Joseph Story, *A Familiar Exposition of the Constitution of the United States* (New York: Harper & Brothers, 1847), 259-61.

[182] D. James Kennedy and Jerry Newcombe, *What if the Bible Had Never Been Written* (Nashville: Thomas Nelson, 1998), 89.

[183] Novak, 16.

[184] Novak, 15.

[185] Barton, *The Role of Pastors & Christians in Civil Government*, 27.

[186] B. F. Morris, *Christian Life and Character of the Civil Institutions of the United States* (Philadelphia: George W. Childs, 1861), 147.

[187] Novak, 92.

[188] Novak, 95.

[189] Hart, 333.

[190] Bill Bright and John Damoose, "Faith of Our Fathers," 9-10.

[191] Hart, 332.

[192] David Azerrad, "What the Constitution Really Says About Race and Slavery," *The Daily Signal*, December 28, 2015, 1.

[193] Donald S. Lutz, "The Relative Influence of European Writers on Late Eighteenth Century American Political Thought," *America Political Science Review*, vol. 78, March 1884, 191; quoted by Barton, *The Role of Pastors & Christians in Civil Government*, 17.

[194] Barton, *The Role of Pastors & Christians in Civil Government*, 18.

[195] John Locke, *The Reasonableness of Christianity* (Stanford: Stanford Univ. Press, 1958), 57

[196] Locke, 57.

[197] Robert Faulkner, *The Jurisprudence of John Marshall* (Westprot, CT: Greenwood Press, 1968), 139.

[198] Noll, 394.

[199] Hart, 306.

[200] When the Founders use the word "religion" they are speaking of Christianity, unless indicated otherwise by the context.

[201] http://www.heritage.org/*research*/lecture/2011/06/did-america-have-a-christian-founding

[202] http://www.straight-talk.net/socas/s-summary.shtml.

[203] James Madison to the General Assembly of the State of Virginia. Some have sought to refute this quote, but it is compatible with Madison's views on government.

[204] Novak, 71-72.

[205] Novak, 72.

[206] Novak, 111.

[207] Hart, 28.

[208] Charles G. Finney, *The Original Memoirs of Charles G. Finney*, Garth M. Rosell & Richard A.G. Dupuis, eds. (Grand Rapids: Zondervan, 2002), 163.

[209] This quote has been historically attributed to Tocqueville, but is not found in any of his writings. It is possible that someone wrote it down from a lecture he gave and it then found its way into circulation.